Intellectual Property: A Very Short Introduction

VERY SHORT INTRODUCTIONS are for anyone wanting a stimulating and accessible way into a new subject. They are written by experts, and have been translated into more than 45 different languages.

The series began in 1995, and now covers a wide variety of topics in every discipline. The VSI library now contains over 508 volumes—a Very Short Introduction to everything from Indian philosophy to psychology and American history and relativity—and continues to grow in every subject area.

Very Short Introductions available now:

Available soon:

GRAVITY Timothy Clifton
VOLTAIRE Nicholas Cronk
MILITARY STRATEGY
Antulio J. Echevarria II

JEWISH HISTORY
David N. Myers
ANIMAL BEHAVIOUR
Tristram D. Wyatt

For more information visit our website

www.oup.com/vsi/

Siva Vaidhyanathan

INTELLECTUAL PROPERTY

A Very Short Introduction

OXFORD
UNIVERSITY PRESS

OXFORD
UNIVERSITY PRESS

Oxford University Press is a department of the University of Oxford.
It furthers the University's objective of excellence in research, scholarship,
and education by publishing worldwide. Oxford is a registered trade mark of
Oxford University Press in the UK and certain other countries.

Published in the United States of America by Oxford University Press
198 Madison Avenue, New York, NY 10016, United States of America.

Library of Congress Cataloging-in-Publication Data
Names: Vaidhyanathan, Siva, author.
Title: Intellectual property : a very short introduction / Siva Vaidhyanathan.
Description: New York : Oxford University Press, 2017. |
Series: Very short introductions
Identifiers: LCCN 2016044875 | ISBN 9780195372779 (paperback)
Subjects: LCSH: Intellectual property (International law) |
Copyright, International. |
BISAC: LAW / Intellectual Property / Copyright.
Classification: LCC K1401 .V33 2017 | DDC 346.04/8—dc23 LC record
available at https://lccn.loc.gov/2016044875

7 9 8

Printed in Great Britain
by Ashford Colour Press Ltd., Gosport, Hants.
on acid-free paper

Contents

List of illustrations

Preface

This book serves three purposes. First, it offers an account of the basic terms of and justifications for the various forms of intellectual property. Second, it sets out the broad contours of debate about the powerful cultural and economic issues that are at work in the world today. And third, it guides curious readers to some of the best recent books, articles, and websites on global intellectual property.

My own travels with intellectual property have been varied and strange. In 1990 I was a newspaper reporter in Texas. I drove up to Taylor, Texas, a small town north of Austin, to interview a young man who was trying to sell packages of condoms that he called "Stealth Condoms." To ensure no one else would market "Stealth Condoms" and drive him out of business, the man filed for trademark protection with the U.S. Patent and Trademark Office. However, lawyers for the giant U.S. defense contractor, the Northrop Corporation, filed a motion to stop the trademark registration. Northrop had developed the B-2 "Stealth" airplane for the U.S. military. In the filing, Northrop's lawyers asserted that the presence of a cardboard package with three condoms—one red, one white, one blue—would "likely cause confusion" in the marketplace.

This was a funny story, but it got me thinking. What public purpose is served by a trademark system that would cause a major defense contractor to spend money on lawyers to stop a young man from selling condoms by mail out of his home? Is the entire trademark system rigged to favor the big and powerful? How can we justify such a system? Does the trademark system benefit society in general or just those companies that were successful and wealthy enough to defend their marks? And how does trademark law fit into the larger concept of "intellectual property?"

Meanwhile, I was making a living producing work that a large media company claimed as its property. What was the role of my labor in the matrix of ownership and creativity? What was my stake in the system? Why didn't I own my own writing? Under what conditions would I? As a reporter I constantly quoted from other published sources. My work often found its way into newspapers far from Austin, Texas, via news services. I even found some reporting I had done on a horrific mass murder in northern Mexico quoted in a cheap exploitive paperback account of the crimes. What justifies that act of borrowing and quoting? How much borrowing is ethical? How much borrowing is legal? And what's the difference between the ethical and legal concerns?

At about the same time I noticed that popular music was changing. Through the 1980s and early 1990s I had been closely following hip-hop music. I was as excited about the creativity, energy, and do-it-yourself spirit of hip-hop in the late 1980s as I had been of punk rock in the early 1980s. By 1991 I noticed that the music had changed. The new work lacked the texture and richness that had marked the finest albums of the late 1980s, such as Public Enemy's *It Takes a Nation of Millions to Hold Us Back* and the Beastie Boys's *Paul's Boutique*. Instead, the digital samples of others' music that made up the intricate bed of sound in those great albums was replaced by a thinner, less interesting, less intricate collection of more obvious samples. The language of sampling seemed to become simpler and less interesting. There was less play and less depth to the music by 1992. I knew that several hip-hop artists had faced copyright suits over sampling in 1990 and 1991. So I wondered if the law had had such a profound effect on the art. After a bit of research, I concluded that it had. With a bit more research, I sought to explain the larger, longer relationship between copyright and creativity in American history. That project became the reason I quit the newspaper business and entered graduate school. And it became the germ of my first book, published in 2001, *Copyrights and Copywrongs: The Rise of Intellectual Property and How It Threatens Creativity.*

By 2001 copyright had exploded into public consciousness, largely through the remarkable rise and fall of Napster, the first easy-to-use digital file-sharing service. The United States had radically expanded copyright law in the 1990s in anticipation of the "digital moment." But nothing had prepared the copyright industries for the torrent of unauthorized peer-to-peer distribution over the Internet, starting in about 2000. Meanwhile, computer software had blossomed from a mere hobby to a multibillion-dollar global industry in the 1980s and 1990s without any clear sense of how intellectual property would work for it (or against it). At about the same time that U.S. courts ruled that software could enjoy the protection of patent law as well as copyright, the movement to lock computer code open for the benefit of security, stability, quality, and creativity (and, to some, humanity) grew to be called the "Free and Open-Source Software" movement. As someone thrown into the copyright battles of the early twenty-first century despite my training as a nineteenth-century cultural historian, I felt compelled to make sense of these and other trends that were remaking our global information ecosystem. Those interests are reflected in my second book, published in 2004, *The Anarchist in the Library: How the Clash between Freedom and Control Is Hacking the Real World and Crashing the System.*

The copyright wars of the first decade of the twenty-first century yielded a global "Free Culture" movement, with law professor Lawrence Lessig as its intellectual leader. Globally, others concerned with issues beyond copyright and creativity, including biopiracy and the cost of pharmaceuticals in developing nations, launched the "Access to Knowledge" movement. During the decade the industries devoted to expanding and strengthening intellectual property succeeded in legislatures and courts around the world. And the United States embedded intellectual property standards into trade treaties with other nations. The issues were becoming more interesting and important every week.

Then, in late 2004 Google announced it would begin to scan into electronic form millions of books from dozens of university libraries—many of which would still be covered by copyright. The ensuing debate and lawsuits drew me into the fascinating world of search engines, Internet policy, and the future of libraries and books. That research generated my third book, published in 2011, *The Googlization of Everything and Why We Should Worry.*

But my relationship with the diverse field of practices, norms, laws, and regulations that we imprecisely call "intellectual property" is not the story I want to tell with this *Very Short Introduction.* Instead, I want to tell your story—or rather—our story.

If you are one of the relatively few people on Earth with the disposable income to purchase this book and the skills and leisure time to read it, then you are already deeply implicated in most forms of "intellectual property." If you receive and send email, text messages, or post to social media services, you are a copyright holder and likely a copyright infringer. If you paid a premium for the latest "smart" phone, then a substantial portion of that price went to pay to enforce patents held by the company that made your phone or—just as likely—paid to license patents owned by another company. Perhaps a portion of your cost paid for a judgment or settlement in a patent infringement case between makers of mobile phones. If you took an over-the-counter allergy medicine today you most likely paid a fraction of the price you would have paid for the same medicine back in 1994 when many of the most popular remedies were still covered by patents and were available only at very high cost via prescription in much of the world. And if you recently purchased a hammer, a ladder, a hose, or a toaster, then you participated in a part of the global economy in which no one owns the design of such common and now old devices. But companies such as Stanley, Black and Decker, and Krups aggressively "brand" these common items with their protected trademarks in hope of convincing us that there is some dependable level of quality inherent in their tools.

The world economy increasingly invests time and money in intangible, aesthetic, entertaining, or smartly designed products, and so "intellectual property" becomes a bigger part of the price we pay for each item we buy—a sort of lawyer tax or "innovation" tax. It also becomes a subject of policy debate the world over. After all, when the wealthy nations of the world design and market medicine that could save thousands of lives every day in those parts of the world lacking the cash to pay for those medicines, we all have to ask ourselves what sort of economy we should design for the world that might meet our health and economic needs as well as our ethical and moral obligations.

This book is intended for a global audience. But my knowledge is biased by my nationality and experience. Many of the stories and issues in this book rely on developments in the United States. Nonetheless, I have tried my best to relate these issues to more general and global trends. If I have done my job, you will close this book more curious about these issues that you were when you picked it up.

Chapter 1

How to read Starbucks, or why intellectual property matters more than you think

I'm writing this in a Starbucks shop in Charlottesville, Virginia. Every Starbucks in the world is recognizable, even though the stores are not identical. Some have beige wooden chairs and tables. This one has dark furniture. Most, but not all, have green trim painted on the walls and doors. This one has large sepia-toned posters of various coffee-brewing technologies. And being Charlottesville, the home of Thomas Jefferson, a large portrait of the former president hangs here with a historical note about his relationship to coffee: The first patent granted for a coffee grinder in the United States was issued to Jefferson's dentist, Thomas Bruff.

The design of every Starbucks is guided by theme and variation. The common thematic elements of the ideal Starbucks include calming music played at a comfortable volume, soft lighting that allows for reading, and staff wearing green aprons. Every Starbucks strives to be visually and aurally calming—or at least comforting. Beyond specific design elements, the very predictability of the design generates comfort among users. Yet variation is just as important. Starbucks stores are designed to speak to the local as well as the global—thus the Jefferson portrait.

When we enter a Starbucks anywhere in the world we share a cosmopolitan space with everyone else in a Starbucks anywhere in the world. We are told by the design to be present, yet connected to the larger world (Internet connectivity and global newspapers help). We use the caffeine to feel energized and engaged, yet the music, lighting, and seating tell us to relax. We are invited to purchase coffee beans from Africa, South America, or Indonesia in forms and sizes marked by Italian words. American jazz and rhythm and blues float from speakers all over the world. And the name and logo of Starbucks is quintessentially American. For a few minutes in the day you can step just outside Charlottesville, Chicago, Caracas, or Cairo. You can just be in the Republic of Starbucks. How does Starbucks do this?

Starbucks sells food and beverages in more than sixty countries. It grew from a local Seattle roaster established in 1971 into a global behemoth by the end of the twentieth century by introducing gourmet coffee and espresso to parts of the world heretofore untouched by anything more flavorful than Nescafé. Starbucks grew big and wealthy by creating, leveraging, and managing intellectual property.

The company has paid close attention to the "trade dress," or design elements of its stores, ensuring that competing coffee outlets do not mimic it too closely. It based its trademarked name and logo on a character from a nineteenth-century American novel that is in the public domain and thus no longer protected by any intellectual property: "Starbuck" was the first mate on the whaling ship *Pequod* in Herman Melville's *Moby Dick*. The "faux-talian" names that Starbucks gives its sweetened drinks ("Fizzio" and "Frappuccino") also are trademarked.

At the front counter of this Starbucks store one can purchase compact discs with music that Starbucks has determined appeals to the clientele of this particular region or store. Starbucks runs its own music publishing company, so it licenses compositions and recordings from artists and other labels. Artists as well known as Paul McCartney, Alanis Morissette, and Carly Simon have signed deals to release albums through Starbucks's Hear Music label.

The company's entertainment production wing, Starbucks Entertainment, produced and distributed, among other works, the 2006 film *Akeelah and the Bee*. And Starbucks has a deal with Apple to distribute iTunes music via its wireless network in stores.

Most striking is the simple beige cardboard "sleeve" that Starbucks provides to shield my sensitive hand from the heat radiating from my cup of Tazo Awake tea. As one would expect, the sleeve carries the trademarked logo, a green outline of a mermaid with a star in her crown. And it displays the trademarked typeface name of the company on one side of the sleeve. The other side of the sleeve carries the numbers of three patents that Starbucks has secured for this "invention." One patent number covers the United States, another Canada, and a third the United Kingdom. "Related foreign patents and foreign patent applications pending," the sleeve reads. The U.S. patent number 6863644 does not cover the sleeve itself. Insulating sleeves are covered by a slew of other patents. According to the application documents on file with the U.S. Patent and Trademark Office, this patent protects: "A machine and method for producing beverage container holders of consistently high quality at high production rates and at an economical cost is disclosed herein." Consider how many lawyer work hours are embedded in this simple piece of corrugated cardboard. Starbucks lawyers were part of the design process and the marketing discussions. They oversee the filing of trademarks and vigilantly enforce these patents and trademarks. A few years ago the Starbucks sleeve design also carried a copyright notice, as if there were copyrightable text worth protecting on the sleeve.

There are two lessons we can take from looking at a local Starbucks as a text to examine intellectual property. First, Starbucks is just as much an intellectual property company as it is a food-and-beverage company. And second, one reason your latte costs so much at Starbucks is that a good portion of the price pays for all the lawyers who protect that cardboard sleeve and everything else that is special about Starbucks's presentation.

1. The sleeve that insulates a hot cup at a Starbucks store in Charlottesville, Virginia, has the markings of copyright, patents, and trademarks.

Intellectual property is a core function of the cultural elements from which we build meaning and of the commercial ecosystem that fuels so much human activity. And Starbucks has mastered both dynamics.

That's not to say that managing Starbucks's rise and intellectual property assets has been easy. Back in 1999 Starbucks opened its first store in China and quickly registered its most valuable trademarks in China, including its name in Mandarin, Xingbake, which sounds a lot like the Chinese word for "star" and the sound of "bucks." Predictably, imitators soon sprang up around China, hoping to capitalize on the growing upper middle class and its expanding luxury consumption habits. One company tried to use the name "Xingbake," claiming that it had registered the trademark before Starbucks did. A Chinese court ruled in 2005 that the Chinese imitator had violated a 2001 law prohibiting the use of another company's trade dress and marks. This was a major test of the new law and marked a step toward fuller integration of the cultural as well as commercial ecosystems of China and the

United States. That case sent a signal to other foreign companies that China might be a safe place to conduct consumer commerce on a massive scale. Various forms of piracy still dominate the cultural markets of China.

Starbucks also has tried to prevent other forms of intellectual property from raising the wholesale prices it pays or inhibiting the ways it wants to conduct business. In 2007 Ethiopia moved to register as trademarks several of its most popular local versions of coffee beans, including Sidamo, Harrar, and Yirgecheffe. Starbucks moved to block the registration in the United States. Ethiopia was attempting to go beyond the established system of geographic origin protection that will be explored later in this book. If Ethiopia were to achieve trademarks for these bean sources, companies like Starbucks and many smaller shops and distributors would have had to pay license fees to call the coffee by its name. This could have returned more money to coffee farmers—or at least to the Ethiopian government. So it would cost Starbucks and other distributors significantly more to use and boast of those sources. After much negotiation and considerable public criticism by Oxfam and other human rights activists and organizations, Starbucks agreed to withdraw its opposition to Ethiopia registering trademarks for the origins and agreed to promote the beans in its stores and pay a premium for them.

Starbucks was able to market the switch as an exercise in corporate social responsibility. It raised its coffee prices soon after and was able to boast to its upscale customers that buying branded beans from Ethiopia was helping bolster the incomes of poor farmers. Ethiopia's effort to trademark traditional agricultural products is an experiment in redressing some of the power imbalances in global commodity trade that have left much of Africa on the losing side of the balance for about 400 years. With every new assertion of an intellectual property right someone pays a higher price for the good or service. The new money did not make the farmers any wealthier, as Starbucks and the Ethiopian government had predicted. But a model of how to conduct global trade had certainly changed.

Reading Starbucks as an intellectual property text is helpful. But it is not the only company that has managed to leverage a tangle of rights into a presence in global culture and commerce. Coca Cola demonstrated the power of a global trademark many decades ago. Pharmaceutical companies use their patent and trademark power to keep prices high on the medications they try to sell globally—despite very different medical needs and abilities to pay across the globe. Publishers like Bertelsmann (the German owners of Penguin Random House and other major imprints) and the *New York Times* try to navigate different cultural norms and copyright traditions, while the World Wide Web spreads its own set of expectations about the availability and cost of content, signaling to its users that content should be available, instantly and at no marginal cost. Companies in China and the United States increasingly team up for "co-production" of major global action films, in part to limit piracy in China. People around the world are building new cultural practices and products using the signs and symbols available to them commercially and otherwise. Intellectual property laws complicate and perhaps impede this sort of cultural play that enriches daily life. And, perhaps most seriously, a growing global movement aims to increase the "access to knowledge" that every resident of the planet can enjoy. Every assertion of an intellectual property right is also a restriction on what others can do or say. Understanding the intellectual property ecosystem demands a full acknowledgment of the justifications for these systems of law and practice and an account of their consequences—positive and negative.

Justification

Imagine a world without intellectual property laws. It could be a nightmare. The medicine you get from the pharmacy could be sugar pills, shaped and marked up to look like the name brand your doctor prescribed. Drug companies would focus on proven products, even if they had to sell them cheaply, rather than investing in risky research, testing, development, and marketing of new treatments. The next sip of Coca-Cola you take could poison you because someone concocted a cheap brown liquid and placed it in bottles marked with the familiar red logo. A laboratory in Korea that invents an efficient electric cell suitable to replace diesel engines in large trucks would opt to keep the technology secret until it can find a vendor, thus robbing others of important basic knowledge that fostered the technological breakthrough. Major recording artists might cease releasing their work in high-quality, mass-marketed forms, and instead rely on amateur recording, rough production quality, informal networks of promotion, and constant live performance to financially justify the work they do. And no more epically expensive superhero movies would emanate from Hollywood. Millions of people in the creative industries would lose their jobs as investors would flee markets that they couldn't predict or trust. And this book might never have been professionally edited, designed, published, marketed, or distributed in such a lovely form.

But a world without intellectual property might not be a total dystopia, either. The cost of essential existing pharmaceuticals would drop to levels that would allow billions more people around the world to afford them. Governments might step up to fund and regulate almost all drug research through public universities and laboratories. Coca-Cola might go out of business after a few poisonings, but people would drink more sugar-free, caffeine-free, and color-free water. Obesity and type II diabetes might wane. New and profound inventions could find their way to market— and knowledge about them could flow faster—through means of disclosure more open and efficient than the current patent system. Artists might abandon the fantasy of striking it rich with a major-label global hit, and fans could reward performers who have mastered their crafts rather than those with major marketing machines behind them. Small-time video makers could deploy the cheap and powerful editing and animation tools available for the personal computer to fill our lives with diverse and lively expressions. The money currently pumped into the major creative industries might spread more equitably, rewarding real creativity rather than inefficient, top-heavy multinational corporations. And I still might have written this book, only to eschew this esteemed publishing house for an open and free distribution system in hopes that readers would appreciate my work enough to leave a nice tip.

Of course, it's rare that someone seriously argues for intellectual property nihilism. Our challenge, as we examine and assess the intellectual property systems at work in the world today, is to create and maintain the positive results of intellectual property while limiting the negative. We want new pharmaceuticals to help us live better and longer. But we want more than wealthy people to be able to live better and longer as well. We would like the occasional summer blockbuster Hollywood (or Bollywood or Nollywood) film. But we would also like witty and brilliant homemade parodies of such films to show up on YouTube.

The world we actually occupy already suffers from many of the maladies of an intellectual-property-free state. It also benefits from many of the lovely aspects of light, irrelevant, or unenforceable laws. Major films are available on street corners and computer screens around the world within hours of their release in Los Angeles. Musicians have seen many of their traditional revenue sources dry up as others rise insignificantly. Knockoff drugs cost many lives already. The United Nations estimates that as many as half of the anti-malarial drugs distributed in Africa are fake. Meanwhile, firms in India and Brazil have been producing anti-retroviral drugs for the developing world over stern opposition from the United States, the European Union, and the major global pharmaceutical companies.

No one is happy with the status quo. Global health activists criticize big pharmaceutical companies for keeping their medicines too expensive for too long. And the companies complain about unauthorized generic versions of their drugs undermining the market and thus harming their ability to fund further research and development. Film and recording companies around the world worry that too many of their products are available for no cost through electronic networks or sold on street corners from Shanghai to São Paulo. Yet the very copyright laws that these companies wrote and promoted often stifle legitimate activities such as research, scholarship, journalism, and creative remixing of hallmarks of global culture.

Since about the turn of the twenty-first century we have seen competing political visions for what sort of global information ecosystem we should have: one committed to the desires of firms that fund and promote expensive goods and expressions or one that serves the interests of the broadest collection of humanity without regard to wealth or cultural status. Industries have lobbied for stronger, broader, and longer intellectual property protections. The "Access to Knowledge" movement has promoted a lighter, more democratic vision of information flow and creativity. Of course, it is not that simple or straightforward. Major firms such as Google (now a part of its holding company, Alphabet) have lobbied for lighter copyright protections largely because a wilder, livelier Web benefits the company that effectively manages the Web in much of the world. And many indigenous cultural groups have advocated for a new form of intellectual property protection to prevent multinational corporations from exploiting "traditional knowledge" without regard for the dignity and integrity of the group.

Is "intellectual property" a useful term?

Despite the centrality of intellectual property policy to so many aspects of the global economy and daily life, it remains one of the most confusing, arcane, and misunderstood subjects. The very phrase "intellectual property" is a source of so much confusion. The phrase is as contested as it is ubiquitous. It stands in for a complex tangle of laws, policies, and values that govern the dissemination of ideas, expressions, inventions, creativity, and data collection. Each area of law that sits under the umbrella of "intellectual property" has its own justification, history, and core values. These areas of law often work at cross-purposes. Yet in public discourse, "intellectual property" stands as a general and undifferentiated regulatory system that prevents some people from using the fruits of others' intellectual work. This unfortunate conflation has caused widespread misunderstanding about the law and who may benefit from it.

The first problem with the phrase is that it conflates so many distinct areas of law and practice that have different historical roots and perform different functions. Copyright and patent are closely related historically. And both systems were designed to serve as incentive systems for creativity and invention. Trademarks and trade secrets serve to protect the reputation and inner workings of companies but do not work as incentive systems. Too often we throw around the phrase "intellectual property" when we should be more precise.

Second, the phrase rhetorically appeals to the notion that these areas of legal protection work like real property. Real property exists, of course, only because the state backs up and sometimes manages claims to ownership—just like with copyright, trademarks, or patents. A major difference exists, however, between real property and these modes of ownership. Real property is called rivalrous. Intellectual property is non-rivalrous. If I own two oranges and another person—a rival—takes one orange from me without permission, then my rival has reduced my supply of oranges by 50 percent and done me real harm. If I write a poem and someone makes a copy of that poem without my permission, I still have the poem. The harm I might suffer is speculative and based on a prediction that I could sell the rights to that poem on a market. I am a horrible poet. No one should pay to license my poems. So copying my poem would do me no real harm. In fact, it might make me feel a bit better that at least one person liked the poem enough to copy it. Rights over rivalrous property are about managing scarcity. Rights over non-rivalrous things are about creating artificial scarcity where scarcity would not naturally exist. "He who receives an idea from me, receives instruction himself without lessening mine; as he who lights his taper at mine, receives light without darkening me," Thomas Jefferson wrote to his friend Isaac McPherson about intellectual property, encapsulating the idea of non-rivalrousness.

You might have noticed that I have gone back to deploying the phrase "intellectual property" to describe the subjects of this book. That is because, despite my misgivings about its misuse and misunderstandings, it still serves as a useful expression for scholarly investigation and legal education. That's why the phrase is in the title of this book. When someone searches for "intellectual property" in a library or bookstore I want her to be able to find this book. But it's also worth conceding that in many important ways the phrase "intellectual property" is a useful description of an interrelated set of phenomena. Copyrights and patents did emerge at roughly the same time in England and Europe. They were both functions of a desire to reward or incentivize creators who would soon spark a series of commercial and industrial revolutions. And, in the case of Starbucks, the blending, merging, and coordination among copyright, trademark, and patent have become common and unavoidable practice that affect daily life and commerce around the world.

Patents, trademarks, and copyrights

There are three main branches of intellectual property law in most of the world: patent, trademark, and copyright law. In recent years, a fourth area, trade secret law, has grown in importance as a way of rewarding commercial innovations outside the public licensing schemes that patent and copyright law employ. In addition, most industries that deal in intellectual property contractually constrain their participants such that contract law becomes de facto intellectual property law. Lately, efforts have been undertaken to create new types of intellectual property law to handle new practices and technologies such as architecture, semiconductor design, and database production. Each of these branches of what has become known as intellectual property law has distinct forms and functions, but many people blend their terms and purposes when discussing intellectual property.

While copyright encourages the dissemination of creative and informative work, patent law encourages invention. Patents grant a temporary monopoly to an inventor of a tangible, useful and "nonobvious" device or process. Patents cover devices and processes, not words, texts, or phrases. In contrast, trademark law lets a company protect and enjoy its "goodwill" in the marketplace. A trademark is some specific signifier—such as a logo, design, color scheme, smell, sound, or container shape—that points to the product's origin. Of these areas of law, copyrights and patents are most frequently conflated. Here's an easy way to distinguish between them: Copyrights are for poems; patents are for mousetraps.

Copyrights and patents share a foundational idea. They are both intended to establish incentives to create and bring to market otherwise expensive things. Both systems allow the state to create temporary, limited monopolies over expressions (under copyright) or ideas and plans (under patent). Both systems grew out of British common law and later were embedded among the first few duties that the U.S. Constitution imposed on the U.S. Congress. Yet in both structure and practice these two areas of law are very different. There is one major area of creativity and commerce in which discrete creations are covered by both patent and copyright law: Computer software. This double-coverage has been controversial since the dawn of the commercial software industry in the 1970s. And it remains an area of hot debate. Should software be covered by either system? Computer algorithms are not quite poetry and they are not quite mousetraps. After all, code itself does not move hearts or mass.

However, much of the most important code we use to run the Internet itself does not rely on traditional copyright or patent law at all. It is free for the taking and free for the changing. The rise of computer code as a ubiquitous and global language and currency has sparked some of the most interesting debates about the relevance and propriety of copyright and patent law worldwide.

The globalization of intellectual property

In the nineteenth century the United States was a pirate nation. American readers took advantage of the fact that the United States did not respect copyrights issued by other countries to purchase cheap versions of novels by Thomas Hardy and Charles Dickens. Many of the legendary American publishing houses such as Harper Brothers and Henry Holt started as pirate firms. Even as late as the 1920s the early American film industry was a pirate operation. Directors shamelessly borrowed plots and characters from copyrighted plays and novels. And the early days of the software industry in the late twentieth century was dominated by a battle. One side were upstart "hobbyists" and academics who believed that software should flow freely among users and on the other were entrepreneurs such as Bill Gates who hoped to build a fortune from using intellectual property to create artificial scarcity for Microsoft products. Every country, and every industry, goes through periods of preferring weak or no intellectual property because they are more interested in cheap goods and low-cost creativity. Then, as countries grow wealthier and certain industries become powerful exporters of goods they flip their positions on intellectual property and fight for maximum protection. Now the United States is the leading force behind global standardization and maximization of intellectual property protection. Not coincidentally, the export of film, software, and the spread of brands like Starbucks around the world followed a period of deindustrialization. If the United States could not sell as many Chevrolets to the rest of the world, at least it could get people to sit through Spider-Man movies.

By the late twentieth century major economic powers such as Germany, Australia, Japan, and the United States had shifted investment from heavy machinery to semiconductors, software, and cinema. And thus the entire rhetorical (and regulatory) sphere of intellectual property grew in importance. The "copyright industries" (film, music, software, publishing) constitute the second-leading sector of U.S. exports after agriculture. That does not even take into account patent licensing, pharmaceuticals, computer hardware such as mobile phones, and other technology transfer transactions. For this reason, the most powerful economies in the world have a strong interest in embedding strong methods of control and enforcement over emerging economies. The fight over the global standardization of intellectual property has become one of the most important sites of tension and conflict in North-South global relations.

"That ideas should freely spread from one to another over the globe, for the moral and mutual instruction of man, and improvement of his condition, seems to have been peculiarly and benevolently designed by nature, when she made them, like fire, expansible over all space, without lessening their density in any point, and like the air in which we breathe, move, and have our physical being, incapable of confinement or exclusive appropriation," wrote Jefferson in that 1813 letter to his friend McPherson. His words capture the motivation behind the "Access to Knowledge" movement, one conceived by activists and scholars around the globe who have grown concerned that the efforts to strengthen, broaden, and lengthen intellectual property protection work against the very enlightenment goals that Jefferson professed. With access to knowledge at low (or no) marginal cost and in forms easy to use and build upon, people can freely explore new forms of expression and invention. They can use the best knowledge around to improve their methods of farming and healing. In a world in which knowledge need not be naturally scarce, the Access to Knowledge Movement pushes back against efforts to maximize the commercial potential of intellectual property. Who will get to control the terms of all this amazing data, music, video, medicine, and technology that fills our lives? Will everyone in the world benefit from these changes or just the wealthy? And will these systems collapse because too few people respect it or understand it?

Chapter 2
Copyright, culture, and commerce

If you write emails to people and post photos and videos to Instagram or YouTube, you are a copyright holder. If you sing at Karaoke bars, read to your child, or share stories from the daily newspaper over Facebook, you are a copyright user. Copyright is the most pervasive cultural regulatory system in the world. It affects the quality of our schools, our public culture, our religious lives, and the cost of the computers and devices that you use in so many aspects of your life. Merely by acting as an active cultural human, most of us are deeply implicated in the copyright system.

Until 2015, if you sang "Happy Birthday to You" to your child, you were a copyright infringer—at least that's what Warner/Chappell Music Inc. would have had you believe. The music publishing company had been charging filmmakers and restaurants for the use of the song in movie scenes and birthday parties for decades. In his situation comedy *Sports Night*, writer and producer Aaron Sorkin wrote an entire episode about one of the characters getting a fictional television network in big legal trouble for singing "Happy Birthday to You" to another on the air (Sorkin's father, Bernard Sorkin, was a copyright lawyer for Time Warner Communications, then the owner of Warner/Chappell Music, and thus had the job of protecting the copyright claim over the song).

It turns out that the song was in the "public domain," namely that collection of works and expressions that exist beyond the reach of copyright ownership and thus serve as a cultural "commons" for all of humanity to use and reuse. No one had ever checked on the matter before about 2010. People just took Warner/Chappell's word that the company owned the copyright to the song. It had been earning up to $2 million per year from royalties on the song. In 2010 law professor Robert Brauneis published the results of an extensive investigation of the copyright status of the song and found that, among other technical problems with copyright claim, the song was first copyrighted in its present form with its present lyrics in 1935. That copyright was never renewed when it expired in 1962. As a result of the research by Brauneis, Warner/Chappell faces a lawsuit in an attempt to recover millions of dollars that people have paid to the company for permission to use the song. In 2015 a U.S. federal court ruled no evidence exists that Warner/Chappell ever held the rights to the song. And because there are no other claimants to the rights, it is assumed the song is in the public domain. In 2016 Warner/Chappell agreed as part of a settlement with those it had charged for the song to pay $14 million in retribution. Few songs are as well known or as frequently sung as "Happy Birthday to You." It's one of the few songs whose words we can count on everyone knowing at a child's birthday party. People are often surprised to learn that Warner/Chappell claimed that the song belonged to it. With the court ruling, an important part of our culture has been restored to the "commons."

If "Happy Birthday to You" were written today, it would have no such complications. The copyright on it would exist as soon as it were written. And it would last seventy years past the death of the songwriter. There would be no renewal of the initial copyright term. So it would not enter the public domain for many, many years without anyone doing anything about it. Copyright law has changed significantly in recent decades. It has become stronger, covers more activities, restricts more uses, and lasts longer than ever before. It also has been fairly standardized across the globe through powerful international trade agreements.

Copyright also has been used to regulate things very much unlike books, poems, songs, and maps—the original sort of works that justified the law in the first place. Copyright now regulates all sorts of activities and devices that rely on encryption and computer code. But, just as significantly, copying has become much easier in recent decades. A computer, after all, is a fancy copy machine, capable of distilling light, sound, and keystrokes into compressed digital signals that can be copied infinitely without degradation, edited and remixed in creative ways, and distributed easily across the globe. So now we have high levels of protection and high legal penalties (both criminal and civil) for not only the act of copying, but also for the creation and distribution of software that facilitates copying and sharing. Meanwhile, we have such widespread ease of copying and sharing that the standard practices of the "creative industries" that rose to wealth and power in the late twentieth century no longer apply. Because of copying and copyright, a massive shift has taken place in the ways we encounter, produce, and participate in culture.

The current copyright system makes no one happy. Producers of expensive content bemoan the ease with which we copy and share their creations and the lack of avenues for remuneration. And the users of copyrighted material fear the wrath of lawyers when they wish to participate fully in the cultural dialogue around them. This breakdown in faith and trust in the system should lead us to reexamine the first principles of copyright. Why do we have it? How did it get this way? Is the current system the best possible system for the current and future creative environment? And are the benefits of the copyright system justly distributed or do the wealthy and powerful continue to reap the bulk of the rewards for it at the expense of everyone else?

What copyright does

At its simplest, copyright is the exclusive right to copy. But, of course, nothing is simple. Some works are eligible for copyright protection. Some are not. Copyright extends far beyond the right to copy to include the exclusive right to perform works publicly and generate sequels and toys, among other things, based on the work. And copyright's exclusivity has important limitations as well.

Generally a work is eligible for copyright protection if it is "original," that is, it contains markers of creative decision making by the author or artists. Something raw or common like an alphabetical listing of names would not be eligible for copyright protection. But a song melody that used an alphabetical list of names as lyrics would be. A work must be "fixed in a tangible medium of expression," to quote U.S. copyright law, to qualify for copyright protection. This means that if I stand up in public and speak a poem into the air, it does not enjoy copyright protection. But if I record the sound of speaking it into the air or I type the poem out on a keyboard into a computer hard drive, it immediately enjoys protection. My computer hard drive is a "tangible medium of expression." So is film, photographic paper, concrete, cloth, and the huge slabs of steel that Richard Serra uses to make his sculptures. Back when "Happy Birthday to You" was written, the copyright system in much of the world depended on "formalities"; one had to file forms to register with a government to get protection that would expire in a fixed number of years. So most works were never protected and almost all entered the public domain rather quickly. Filing was too high a burden given the short term of the market value for newspapers or magazines, for instance. But now, since there are no formalities and everything enjoys copyright protection upon fixation, almost everything is protected by default.

The types of works that are eligible for copyright keep growing as new technologies come along. When the United States passed its first copyright law in 1793, the law covered maps, charts, and books. Currently and generally, copyright protects literary works (fiction and nonfiction), musical compositions and lyrics, dramatic works such as plays and scripts, choreography, pictures and sculptures, motion pictures and other audiovisual productions, sound recordings, and architectural designs. This list can be read broadly to include all sorts of digital and analog methods of production and distribution. So if someone invents a new way to present audiovisual material, it would be already covered. Legislators would not have to go back and amend the law every time a new medium arrives.

Once an original work is fixed in a tangible medium of expression, the copyright holder—sometimes an individual, sometimes a group of people, often a corporation—has the exclusive right to do the following things: To reproduce the works; to produce what are called "derivative works," such as sequels, toys, clothes, lunch boxes, and other products inspired by the work; to decide how and where to sell, lease, or lend the work; to perform the work publicly if it is a literary or dramatic work; to display the work publicly if it is a picture or sculpture; and to transmit a sound recording of the work over digital networks.

This is a broad and powerful list of exclusive rights. And by "exclusive," we mean that only the copyright holder hold these rights. But over time courts and legislators around the world have recognized that if these rights are too broad and powerful, then copyright holders could impede some essential functions of culture and democracy. So courts and legislators have poked breathing holes into copyright to allow the public interest to flourish along with copyright.

The limits of copyright

There are four major limitations to the exclusive rights of copyright holders. They vary in strength and relevance around the world.

These limitations are: Expiration, fair use or fair dealing, first sale, and the idea/expression dichotomy. The power and utility of these exceptions varies across the globe. And some of them are quickly shrinking in utility while others are growing.

The first and most powerful limitation on the powers of copyright is expiration. At some point, generally seventy years after the death of the copyright holder (or ninety-five years after publication if the copyright holder is a corporation), the work enters the public domain, where it can be copied and used fully by the public. For most of American history, copyright terms were short and fixed. The first term was for fourteen years, renewable for another fourteen years. By the middle of the twentieth century, the term had lengthened to a maximum of fifty-six years—two terms of twenty-eight years. By the end of the twentieth century, the term in the United States matched the standard set by European law: Life of the owner plus fifty years. And then, in 1998, the United States added twenty more years to all current copyrighted works and extended the term for new works to life of the author plus seventy years. Once a work finally enters the public domain it belongs to all of humanity. The price of copies can drop significantly. New artists and authors may make derivative works.

One would assume that Sherlock Holmes is in the public domain. Arthur Conan Doyle first conjured the character in 1887. His stories have been beyond copyright for many decades. But because Doyle's estate and heirs have fostered posthumous versions of Holmes's stories created by other authors and filmmakers, they have long claimed that some aspects of Holmes's character are newer and thus still covered by copyright. Amazingly, authors and filmmakers have gone along with the estate's demands and paid to license the character. In 2014 an American lawyer, Leslie Klinger, successfully sued to establish that Holmes and his sidekick, Dr. Watson, are alive and well in the public domain. Klinger could then proceed with his planned book, *The New Annotated Sherlock*

Holmes. This happens often, as authors' estates assert rights over the work of the dead. This phenomenon highlights the question at the heart of copyright: For whom does it exist? Is it to benefit the public and thus seed new works, even new works based on older works? Or does it exist to reward heirs who contributed nothing to the creation of the old works in question?

Popular culture is full of outstanding works that have been largely based on older works now in the public domain. The musical *Big River* comes from Mark Twain's *Adventures of Huckleberry Finn*. Leonard Bernstein's *West Side Story* is *Romeo and Juliet*, yet it's so much more. And the most successful commercial film of 2004, *The Passion of the Christ*, is a retelling of the Gospels of Luke and Matthew. Walt Disney and his company built an empire on creating charming versions of public domain works, from *Cinderella* to *Mulan*. These meaningful stories become part of the collective identity of nations and cultures. Membership, or cultural citizenship, depends on one's familiarity with and facility with retelling such stories. One of the reasons that it is important for copyrights to expire is that we need to replenish the public domain with our most powerful stories and characters to allow new artists to make new statements with them. If copyrights lasted forever, then many stories and characters would freeze forever, like Han Solo in carbonite.

Fair use and fair dealing

Han Solo, like the other elements of George Lucas's *Star Wars* series of films, may be used by some people for some select uses, despite the fact that the character and the films in which it appeared will not enter the public domain until at least 2072. In the United States we enjoy "fair use" rights that allow us to use copyrighted works for purposes that enhance the public good. Fair use was designed to facilitate some flexibility in copyright. If every time a film critic wanted to quote a film, she had to ask for permission from the studio, then film criticisms would be both expensive and rare. No film critic has the time or money to clear the rights to small quotes or still images from expensive films. And film producers have no incentive to allow for reviews that might be negative. No teacher could reasonably secure the rights to distribute short articles about events in the world that he saw in that day's newspaper. No parodist could feel safe skewering television shows or celebrities if she could not confidently rely on fair use.

Fair use is fluid and somewhat unpredictable. Some predictable aspects of it have grown out of some strong recent court decisions. But many gray areas of fair use still remain. That's both a boon and a curse. Fluidity and flexibility allow fair use to work in situations and for purposes that no court or legislature has yet imagined. But every time a new use or new copying technology emerges, it is difficult to predict how well fair use will protect users. In the meantime, attracting accusations of infringement can be risky and costly.

The law does offer some guidance that we can use to venture predictions or guesses about whether using an image or a quote in a new work would be considered fair. U.S. law instructs judges to consider the following four factors when judging whether a use is fair:

- The purpose and character of the use to which the copyrighted material is put. This means that a court will favor uses that advance critical, commentary, or educational ventures. It will not favor uses that are purely commercial unless they enhance some other value. We have seen in recent years the rise of a powerful category of use called "transformative use." A work is transformative if it takes the original work or part of the original work and repurposes it significantly to create new meaning or releases new forms of creativity. So, for instance, when the hip-hop group 2 Live Crew recorded a parody of Roy Orbison's classic song "Oh Pretty Woman," Orbison's publisher sued.

In 1994 the U.S. Supreme Court ruled that the new song was clearly a parody of the older and this had sufficiently transformed the earlier. One cannot create a parody of a familiar and established work without referring to it clearly and unmistakably. A year later photographer Annie Leibovitz sued the producers of the film *Naked Gun 33 1/3: The Final Insult*. Leibovitz had made the iconic photograph of actor Demi Moore pregnant, which had appeared on the cover of *Vanity Fair* in 1991. The movie poster for the film featured actor Leslie Nielsen in the exact pose as Moore had taken for the magazine cover. A court ruled that the poster was sufficiently transformative.

- The nature of the original, copyrighted work used. A court would generally favor the use of nonfiction or news-based work over purely creative or artistic work. The idea behind this distinction is that copyright law should not hamper political speech, education, or research.

- The amount or substantiality of the original work. Contrary to many popular assumptions, there is no formula that determines when a use is fair and when it is not. There is no maximum number of words, percentage of a work, length of a song clip, or similar measurement that will certainly be considered fair and non-infringing. If there is a rule of thumb, it is that the user should use no more of the original than is necessary to make the point intended. So if a critic wants to discuss the meaning of two key lines of a poem, she should avoid quoting more than those two lines. Limiting quotation to the core passage may backfire, however. When *The Nation* magazine published just 400 words out a 500-page memoir of former President Gerald Ford, Ford's publisher sued the magazine. Ultimately the U.S. Supreme Court ruled that those 400 words, concerning Ford's justification for pardoning impeached president Richard Nixon, were the "heart of the work." So the lessons users can take from this aspect of fair use are muddied. One should not take more than the important parts of an older work. But it should not be too important.

- The effect of the use on the potential market for the original work. The key to this factor is the "potential" market. Even if the copyright holder has not entered a specific market—say, creating dolls based on characters in a film—another firm may not use the copyrighted work in such a way that denies the copyright holder of entering that market with all the advantages of the copyright monopoly. Of course, many fair uses do affect the market or potential market for the original. A negative review of this book, for instance, would stifle sales and limit my ability to pursue markets for derivative works, like dolls based on major figures in intellectual property history.

It is important to note that the four factors are not exhaustive. Courts will often consider other issues and facts when rendering their decisions. In addition, they are not a checklist or a scorecard. One side does not prevail for "winning" three out of the four factors. So the factors can offer some guidance. But it is best to consider the use in the context of previous cases in which fair use was invoked as a defense.

Fair use emerged from case law in the United States almost two hundred years ago as courts recognized that many reasons could be adduced to allow for limited uses of copyrighted works to flow in the culture for the sake of enhancing democratic speech, education, and political knowledge. Education, journalism, and criticism were public goods that strong copyright could inhibit. In 1976 the U.S. Congress codified fair use in the law. Since then it has grown in stature and now enables not only small, individual uses of copyrighted material, but also large, wholesale uses as well. In the mid-1970s when Sony introduced its consumer video recording machine, the Betamax, it immediately generated the ire of the motion picture industry. Studios filed suit and the case went all the way to the U.S. Supreme Court in 1984. After much disagreement on the court and a five-to-four vote, the justices ruled that Sony could not be held liable for creating a product that could be used by others to infringe on copyrights, and that infringement was not the only purpose of the machine. The video cassette recorder, the court ruled, also had "substantial non-infringing uses" such as letting people record television shows for viewing at a more convenient time, a practice that has become known as "time shifting." This case was significant for several reasons. It made certain that firms could have some confidence to produce machines that could copy promiscuously, yet the firms would not have to police their consumers or be held liable for the things consumers do. Second, the court made clear that certain behaviors en masse were to be considered non-infringing, such as time shifting. Fair use had largely been considered a case-by-case defense against accusations of infringement. But in the Betamax case fair use grew into a general license to record for personal use.

The U.S. Supreme Court further strengthened and expanded the usefulness of fair use in 1994 when it considered whether a parody of Roy Orbison's 1964 pop-country hit "Oh, Pretty Woman." The new song by the group 2 Live Crew, called just "Pretty Woman," used similar lyrical patterns over a bed of hip-hop music. The Court ruled on two important questions that have made significant differences to how fair use works in the twenty-first century. First, a parody of an original work is fair use, largely because a parodist should not be required to ask permission from an artist to mock the artist's work. And second, the Court ruled that 2 Live Crew had sufficiently "transformed" the original into something new. This concept of "transformative use" would go on to provide support to many more examples of new creators explicitly building on earlier work—in some cases by directly copying the work.

Search engines turn copyright upside down

Fair use morphed from a case-by-case and individualized defense into a general right to copy—even for explicitly commercial purposes—through two major cases concerning Internet search engines in the early twenty-first century. And both of these cases depended directly on the right that 2 Live Crew asserted when the group mocked "Oh, Pretty Woman." The first involved copyrighted images posted on the Web. All search engines work by making copies of documents and items on the Web. Once they are copied they are indexed, or tagged and identified, by the search engine software. If search engines could not make copies, they could not make web pages and items available. If they had to seek permission and payment for each image or piece of text they copied, search engine companies would go broke. More likely, they would stop trying to index the entire Web and would focus on certain allowable items. The cost of running search engines would be much higher than they are and they would be less valuable to Web users. So when a photographer named Les Kelly sued an image search engine company called Arriba Soft in 2002 he was asserting a vision of copyright that had long existed: The copyright holder, by default, has the exclusive right to copy the work. Kelly assumed fair use would not protect a commercial entity making copies of an entire artistic work for a profit-making enterprise. That is how copyright works in the rest of the universe, anyway. Arriba Soft's argument prevailed in court, however, because the company had successfully transformed the original into part of a very useful service. The public good was served by enabling Web searching. And Arriba Soft presented only "thumbnails," or small and degraded versions of the original images. So while the full-sized work existed in Arriba Soft's servers, Web users could experience the full image only by clicking on the link Arriba Soft provided and moving to the host site.

Search engines had for years acted as if their practice of indexing the Web was legal. They asserted, correctly, that without such a right we would have no search engines. But until the Arriba Soft ruling in 2002 there was no strong and clear case law in the United States asserting that right. Two years later Google announced that it planned to scan millions of books from what became hundreds of libraries around the world. Many of these books would be under copyright. But the vast majority would be in the public domain. Google's plan was to enable Web users to read and even download public domain works from Google Books service. But for works that might be under copyright Google would allow users to see only the search terms they used within "snippets" of copyrighted text. Google argued that the user would see only a sliver of the entire work. The user could not copy or even reconstruct the entire work from snippets. And Google provided links to sources where users could acquire the book from either libraries or bookstores. Based on the Arriba Soft precedent, Google was confident it would prevail. Publishers were not convinced.

It was one thing for Arriba Soft, Google, Yahoo, and other search engines to scour the Web for digital materials that people had actively made available in digital form. Once these copyright holders had opted into the norms of the Web, they were agreeing to allow their works to be scanned by search engines. After all, why would someone post something on the Web and then wish not to have it found? If, for some reason, a copyright holder objected to having a site indexed by a search engine, the holder could plant a bit of code into the page that would instruct the search engine to move along and ignore that site. So on the Web, massive copying was an opt-out system. One had to act to step back from the default practice of making work available for copying. In the rest of the universe and since the dawn of copyright, copying had been opt-in. The copyright holder could decide when, how, and if work would be made public. If the copyright holder chose not to put the work in a particular form such as a digital file, then it would never assume that form.

The Google Books project turned that upside down. Google was forcing works that had never existed in digital form (or were in the process of taking very different digital forms, such as commercially available ebooks in protected and proprietary formats chosen by the publisher) into digital files, held only on Google servers. Once books were digitized, Google did to them what Arriba Soft had established was legal to do to digitized images posted on an open website: Indexed them and made them available in a lesser form. So the questions were: Did Google satisfy the terms of fair use by limiting how the works would appear to users? Or did Google fundamentally infringe on hundreds of thousands of copyrights by copying the entire works into forms the copyright holders had never agreed to and folding them in to a commercial service?

It took almost a decade of argument, posturing, and almost settling the case between publishers and Google before a federal judge ruled in 2013 that Google Books was a sufficiently transformative use of all those books. So Google would not be not liable for copying them without permission. And the judge dismissed the case. "In my view, Google Books provides significant public benefits," wrote Judge Denny Chin. "It advances the progress of the arts and sciences, while maintaining respectful consideration for the rights of authors and other creative individuals, and without adversely impacting the rights of copyright holders."

Because of the rulings concerning the Sony Betamax recorder, the parody of Roy Orbison's "Oh, Pretty Woman," Web search, and Google Books, U.S. courts significantly have changed how copyright works. These cases all relied on fair use. Fair use is still risky for individuals who hope to make slight uses of copyrighted material, as the threat of a lawsuit—even one without much merit—may cost the user significant time and money. Because of this, a group of scholars at American University in Washington, D.C., have launched a project to establish "best practices" within certain communities of practice that make clear that the norms and expectations of the community allow for certain reasonable uses of copyright material and thus these uses should be considered fair. The group's first successful project involved documentary filmmakers. For decades filmmakers had been stifled when inadvertently capturing copyrighted music, television shows, or images in the background of shots they were taking. People in real life sing copyrighted songs out loud all the time. They watch *The Simpsons* in the background of a living room while discussing their days. They have music playing in bars, barbershops, and cars. Pretending these copyrighted elements of daily life do not exist would violate the ethical tenets of documentary filmmaking. So in the early 2000s filmmakers met with Professors Peter Jaszi and Patricia Aufderheide at American University and forged a list of allowable uses of ambient copyrighted material. Filmmakers use this code of best practices to demonstrate in court that the standard practices allow for such use. This has empowered and emboldened filmmakers to do their work without fear. As such efforts spread, we can see U.S. copyright becoming a bit more flexible.

Fair use, for all its virtues and limitations, is an American thing. It does not apply once a work crosses the border to Canada or Mexico. Many countries, such as Canada, New Zealand, Singapore, India, South Africa, Australia, and the United Kingdom, have a system known as "fair dealing." Fair dealing satisfies many of the same needs that fair use does in the United States: It protects uses of copyrighted material that serve the public interest, such as journalism, criticism, research, and education. The main difference is that fair dealing provisions are enumerated, thus specific to certain tasks. So fair dealing can offer greater confidence to users, but far less flexibility as cultural practices and technologies change. So, for instance, while a court decision made parody qualify as fair use in the United States, the Canadian Parliament had to amend the copyright law in 2010 to add parody as a permitted use under fair dealing. And teachers in Canada may not distribute copyrighted material to their students without clearing it, while that practice is allowed in the United States under some circumstances. Beyond the list of nations that offer fair dealing provisions, many others have enumerated exceptions to the power of copyright. But like so much else in a rapidly globalizing world, such exceptions remain a confusing patchwork and reflect both local values and local political power alignments.

First sale and public lending rights

In the United States copyright owners are permitted to dictate only the terms of the first sale of the copyrighted work. This means that an author (or her publisher after a contract assigns the author's rights) may determine when and how a book reaches the market in hardcover, paperback, electronic text, or audio file. But the law explicitly limits the copyright holder's control over what happens next. A library may purchase the hardcover book. And the library may lend it hundreds or thousands of times. After some time the library staff might decide that the book is no longer in demand and it should be removed from circulation. The library might put the used book up for sale at a price far below its list price. The first sale doctrine prevents the copyright holder from interfering in any of

2. A bookseller offers many used books and magazines to those who stroll along the left bank of the Seine River in Paris. Copyright does not extend to the object itself, so used books may be sold freely without permission from the copyright holder.

these decisions, even though the decision to lend the book might undermine efforts to sell more copies of the book, the decision to remove the book might injure the reputation of the author or book by limiting who might stumble across it, and the decision to sell the used copy would put pressure on the publisher to lower the list price of a new book. The first sale doctrine is what makes libraries and used book stores in the United States possible.

Other countries have different use rights. In Canada, for instance, libraries must pay lending licensing fees through a system known as "public lending rights." These fees are intended to offset the loss from potential sales of the book. The United Kingdom, Germany, Austria, Belgium, Sweden, Norway, Israel, the Netherlands, Australia, New Zealand, and other countries have similar public lending rights programs. In these countries, because libraries are publicly funded, the fees paid to publishers constitute public subsidies of the publishing industry. This is important cultural policy in countries with small populations and small native-language publishing industries, such as Norway or the Netherlands. But the practice is not without harsh criticism from international library associations and others who consider public lending rights programs expensive limitations on the public circulation of knowledge.

The first sale doctrine is easy to enforce with materials sold in physical form, such as books, printed photographs, tapes, and discs. But if a work exists in ephemeral digital form and is delivered over electronic networks then the first sale doctrine gets muddy. The copyright holder might impose contractual terms on the user to grant access in the first place. Those terms might limit the ways that the user might redistribute the digital file, thus undermining any potential for a second sale, lease, gift, or lending. In addition, the publisher could place technological limitations on the file, making it disappear after one reading, viewing, or listening experience. Or the publisher could impose digital locks on the material that would tether the file to one specific machine, thus preventing further distribution. This is certainly the case with electronic books sold by Amazon for its Kindle platform. Amazon will let readers lend titles only under Amazon's terms. And Amazon has been known to delete book files from users' Kindles when Amazon's own contracts limited the company from distributing the title. So as more material is distributed electronically first sale applies less with each new format and delivery system.

The idea/expression dichotomy

Perhaps the most poorly understood aspect of copyright concerns what it does protect and what it does not protect. Copyright protects specific expressions. But it does not protect the facts or ideas that are conveyed by that expression. For this reason, one cannot claim copyright over a simple list of items, facts, or statistics. It also means that different authors and artists may express the same ideas or facts in their own manner and style. The very fact that copyright applies only to matters of manner and style ensures that many people can participate in conversations over a set of ideas and pull from similar influences. This creates a constellation of expressions around a set of ideas. It also means we can choose which film about a meteor heading to destroy Earth we would rather see or which book advocating a low-carbohydrate diet we would rather read. One might be better than the other. If copyright protected facts or ideas, then we would have far fewer versions from which to choose. And we would lack a chain of argumentation or conversation in matters of public policy. If one author uses a set of data to argue for the elimination of public welfare support for the poor, then another author can interpret the data in a very different way and make the opposite case. Public debate would simply not occur if one had to secure permission to use facts.

The confusion that many people hold over this dichotomy is best expressed in the complaint that "he stole my idea." Ideas for patentable works are protected. But ideas underlying creative works are not protected by copyright. They may be protected by other means, however. One way to protect ideas is through the assertion of unfair competition, a tort that implies a second party undermined the first by riding for free on the labor and investment of the first. Often when we read about "plagiarism" lawsuits involving concepts for films the actual legal complaint is unfair competition, not copyright infringement.

Many professional and creative communities have widespread norms against idea theft. Stand-up comics, for instance, police their ranks and punish those who steal jokes from others. Through shunning, reputation sanctions, and the occasional threat of physical force, comics ensure that there is a more efficient and effective system to police such umbrage than copyright law would allow. Ideas are protected within journalism and academia as well. Concern is widespread about plagiarism in both communities. And harsh professional sanctions are in place for the sin of using another's ideas without granting proper credit via standardized methods of citation. But plagiarism is not copyright infringement and copyright infringement is not plagiarism. There can be crossover between these two sets of violations. Copyright is a limited set of legal rights and plagiarism is an ethical abrogation that undermines trust within and beyond an expressive community. One can commit copyright infringement without plagiarizing. And one can plagiarize without infringing copyright. Once can do both, of course. But extralegal sanctions are usually easier to apply.

The many cultures of copyright

Copyright law has been globalized and standardized in many ways since the 1990s. But the difference between fair use and fair dealing systems is not the only residual difference preventing true globalization of copyright. Copyright law's diverse roots still show themselves in the details and styles of enforcement. Two very different historical and philosophical foundations underpin

French and Anglo-American copyright. American copyright was derived from British copyright, specifically the 1710 Statute of Anne, which made clear that copyright was to serve the public interest first, and the rights of authors were merely tools to be employed toward the goal of enriching the public sphere with art and knowledge. If the interests of authors exceeded the interests of the public, and perhaps undermined the interests of the public, then the public interest should prevail in the United Kingdom or United States. In France, copyright sprang from a movement among influential authors and benefited the public only to the extent that great French works would enrich the stature of the nation.

One consequence of this difference is that authors in parts of the world more influenced by French arguments or imperialism enjoy stronger "moral rights" than those in the United States do. If an author has strong moral rights, then she may limit the ways in which her work is presented and by whom, so as not to cast her reputation poorly or imply that her work could be used to endorse a product that she does not believe in. Moral rights do not travel with the assignment of rights to a publisher. So if a publisher purchases all the rights to a book and wishes to create a derivative work, such as a doll or comic book, that degrades the integrity of the work or contains derogatory images, the author in France may block such a move.

In the United States creators have very weak moral rights. So in the 1980s when millionaire Ted Turner purchased the rights to hundreds of classic American films and announced plans to colorize them, film directors, who had no copyright stake in their films, objected loudly. John Huston was particularly upset and tried to block Turner's registration of the American copyright on his film *The Asphalt Jungle*. Having failed to invoke moral rights in the United States, Huston died unsatisfied. Soon after Huston's death in 1988, his daughter, actor Angelica Huston, persuaded a French court to block Turner's plan to show the colorized version of *The Asphalt Jungle* on Channel 5 in France. The most interesting aspect of this case is that Huston was not the "author" of the film. Like most commercial films, Huston made it as a "work made for hire" on behalf of a studio, the original copyright holder. Huston had no legal claim over the film whatsoever under U.S. law. So when a French court agreed to respect his wishes in France—or more precisely, his daughter's wishes, even though Angelica Huston inherited nothing in relation to *The Asphalt Jungle*—ultimately, and after several years and levels of litigation, the Cour de Cassation ruled that under French law all directors are at least co-authors. And thus that status was passed along to Huston's heir.

French law protects four kinds of moral rights: The right of "paternity," or acknowledgment of source; the right of "integrity," which loosely protects the work from being chopped up or misrepresented; the right of "divulgation," or the right to disclose the work; and the right to "repent," or reclaim the work and stop it from being circulated. These are very strong rights that put substantial burdens on resellers, libraries, researchers, and those who would distill the works in ways that the author would find objectionable. Mostly, it binds the publisher from introducing versions of the work that do not conform to the author's vision or wishes. The differences between French-based systems and U.S.-inspired systems still exist, largely because the political power of U.S. film companies has prevented the United States from adopting even flimsy moral rights systems.

Paracopyright

Because copyright has so many limitations and loopholes, even if they are inconsistent across the globe and fluctuate in utility over time, copyright holders have been trying to extend the power of copyright beyond the law itself. They have created "paracopyright" in two ways: contractually and technologically. By requiring purchasers of copyrighted material to agree to terms by which the consumer gives up certain rights, such as fair use or first sale, copyright holders can control more than basic copyright law allows. This is especially effective with digital material. A user agreement, written in complicated legal language in a document too long to expect a consumer to read, could include provisions that prevent users from reading an electronic book aloud, even though most private readings—such as to a child before bedtime—would clearly be allowed under most copyright systems. Sporting events and museums, for instance, try to assert contractual limitations on what patrons may record and transmit. Patrons might have to agree pursuant to purchasing a ticket and entering the premises that they will not take photographs of works of art, even if those works are old enough to be in the public domain.

Contractual restrictions that extend the power of copyright can be further strengthened by technological restrictions. Many digital media files, including digital video discs (DVDs) and books for the Amazon Kindle reader, come encased with encryption that allows

3. A child at the Musée Granet in Aix-en-Provence copies a painting that is in the public domain.

only authorized players to unleash the content. It would take the application of a small batch of computer code to unlock this "digital rights management" (DRM) system. But in the United States a law signed in 1998 called the Digital Millennium Copyright Act prohibits the creation and distribution of any technological method that could circumvent digital rights management systems. Many other countries have followed the United States in granting strong legal protection to digital protections.

Digital rights management has the potential to tip the balance of copyright entirely in favor of the copyright holder. Technological restrictions do not expire. They can be used to protect works already in the public domain. They do not step out of the way for researchers, students, teachers, or critics to make fair use of the copyrighted material. And more often than not digital rights management is used to tether the content to a particular device, thus limiting the ability to lend or resell the work and undermining the first sale doctrine. The prohibition against circumventing digital rights management also puts a burden on librarians and archivists who might want to preserve copies. There are often legal exemptions to the law for librarians and archivists to perform such work. But the very tools necessary to unlock the content for preservation are still against the law. In recent years many media companies have found that they do not have the wherewithal to police all the various ways people have figured out to circumvent the protection measures around content. So digital rights management usage is on the wane. Or at least it is no longer considered the panacea for the copyright industries that it once was. Still, the law strongly favors the interests of copyright industries, and the combination of contract and technology have at least limited competition in some industries and limited how consumers may make legitimate use of the content they have lawfully acquired.

The political battles over copyright started in the late 1990s. Copyright industries saw the emerging networked digital environment as both a serious threat—because everyone would soon own a connected copy machine—and an opportunity—because digital rights management could allow companies to govern use of and charge fees for their works as never before. During the early part of the twenty-first century, as peer-to-peer networks allowed people everywhere to share millions of audio and video files for free, the content companies went on the legal offensive. Music and film companies successfully sued companies like Napster and Grokster that distributed the platforms that allowed for such sharing. And the music industry began a series of high-profile threats and lawsuits against people it accused of sharing music. These tactics created significant backlash in public opinion and ultimately did little to boost either revenue or faith in copyright. By the second decade of the twenty-first century the individual lawsuits had ceased and peer-to-peer networks continued rolling, only occasionally facing criminal or civil charges in egregious and high-profile cases.

By 2017 many of the leading thinkers and policymakers working with global copyright had concluded that it was time to rethink the entire system. That conversation has yet to occur. And if it does, it will pit many of the world's most influential companies against some of the world's most entrenched cultural habits. But the copyright status quo is a mess. Something so central to our economy and culture should not be so opaque, so captured by special interests, and so unpredictable.

Chapter 3
Patents and their discontents

In his 1889 novel *A Connecticut Yankee in King Arthur's Court*, Mark Twain has his protagonist, the inventor, and (as we would call him now) entrepreneur, Hank Morgan take a blow to the head. Morgan awakes to find himself stranded centuries before his birth, in medieval England during the reign of King Arthur. Through a series of machinations involving the invocation of scientific facts and basic technologies that were common among late-nineteenth-century Connecticut Yankees, Morgan quickly assumes control over the administration of England. Morgan never becomes king. Instead, his commercial orientation yields a different honorific: The Boss.

Once Boss, Morgan mentions in passing that "the very first official thing I did, in my administration—and it was on the very first day of it, too—was to start a patent office; for I knew that a country without a patent office and good patent laws was just a crab, and couldn't travel any way but sideways or backways." Twain used Morgan to celebrate and satirize the commercial-technological ideology that dominated his time and nation. The dominant ideology of the United States in the early twenty-first century is not so different from what it was in Twain's Gilded Age. And, in fact, establishing a patent office was among the first things Congress did after the ratification of the U.S. Constitution in 1789. Much of the rest of the world has been more reticent to establish patent systems. Only recently have most countries conformed to U.S.-dictated norms and standards of patent protection. But to this day no truly global patent system exists. Some treaties ensure that there is mutual respect for patents. But unlike copyright, patents must be registered in individual nation-states to ensure maximum protection. Why did Morgan insist that creating a patent system was the first thing he had to do in King Arthur's court? What was he trying to accomplish? Morgan affirms that a country without a patent system could not progress. But what does "progress" really mean? And was Morgan correct?

How do patents work?

A patent is a state-granted limited monopoly. The patent system is intended to create an incentive to create, invent, and market inventions to, in the words of the U.S. Constitution, "promote the sciences and useful arts." A patent grants the holder (not always the inventor) the exclusive right to manufacture, use, sell, or build upon the covered technology. In the United States, the term of patent protection is currently twenty years, after which the invention enters the "public domain" where it is free to use by anyone. Being in the public domain does not remove a technology from the market. After all, firms still sell hammers. But it does remove the ability to charge monopolistic prices and exclude others from using the technology. In the public domain, a technology is open to all. In addition to real-world physical inventions, the U.S. patent system allows firms to control software, business methods, therapeutic processes, and—for a while and until recently—some natural phenomena. These have been among the most controversial recent developments in patent law and policy. A patent monopoly lasts a much shorter time than copyright does—twenty years compared to life of the author plus seventy years for copyright—but it protects more broadly. A patent protects the ideas, as well as the specific invention itself, so that a similar invention that operates along the same lines as the protected invention would be considered an infringement. Patent law, unlike copyright, protects the idea behind an invention, not just the specific design.

The patent system developed first in fifteenth-century Italy, and it spread slowly to other European countries over the next four centuries. These patents were generally royal proclamations of monopoly control, meant to ensure loyalty, curry favor, or ensure a cut of revenue for the court. By 1623, King James I of England had recognized that technological advances could yield military and economic advantage, so he, at the behest of Parliament, began granting fourteen-year patents for inventions and encouraging trade and technological espionage. In the early days of the United States, the founders remained wary of state-granted monopolies, so they built limits into the U.S. patent system to capture the "balance" between the incentive to invent and the public good.

Patents, copyrights, and trademarks all regulate the virtual and replicable—that for which there is no natural scarcity. For markets to operate efficiently and predictably and to prevent the price of ephemeral goods from approaching zero because of rampant replication, wealthy states have in recent years begun to increase the scope, levels, and duration of protection of intellectual property. This process has generated much pain and profit. Like other forms of intellectual property, patent law has been the subject of intense global debate. Because patent laws govern the ability of pharmaceutical companies to fix prices, they are under scrutiny for keeping essential medications out of the reach of the poorest, sickest people in the world. Because patents may capture natural biological resources that poor people have exploited for centuries and multinational companies have processed and brought to market, they are a controversial element in what critics in the developing world call "biopiracy." And because patents on software have the power to limit the use of certain algorithms, many in the software community have criticized their persistence in the United States and have tried to block their entry in the European patent system.

To acquire a patent in the United States, an inventor must file documents with the U.S. Patent and Trademark Office. While reviewing a patent application, inspectors employ three tests to determine the viability of the invention:

- Is the invention useful? Does it actually do something?

- Is the invention original? Is there "prior art" on the record that would show that someone has already brought such a technology to market?

- Is the invention "non-obvious?" Would such a development be beyond the imagination of every reasonable practitioner of the art or science?

These seem like common-sense standards, but they have been far from simple to enforce. A patent application can take many months for approval or (in increasingly rare instances) rejection. Teams of specialized agents work for the patent office in diverse areas of expertise such as chemistry, pharmaceuticals, metallurgy, and software. They are supposed to screen each application to ensure that the invention meets the three basic criteria. Much of their work involves researching previous patent documents for "prior art" that might show that the application does not meet the standard of originality. Often, examiners will send the application back to the applicant for revision so that it does not overlap in scope with "prior art," namely a technique or technology that is already known of or in use within the industry.

Once a patent has been granted, it must be enforced and defended through the judicial system. In the United States, all patent claims since 1983 have gone through a specially designated court called the Court of Appeals for the Federal Circuit. This court rules in cases of infringement or overlap. It has generally broadened and deepened the rights of established patent holders, significantly lowering the threshold of patentability. As a result, the number of patents issued in the United States has increased at an annual rate of 5.7 percent since 1982. By contrast, patents rose at a rate of less than 1 percent per year from 1930 through 1982. The owner of a patent has many powers over the technology. The patent may be sold to others, may be used as collateral for loans, may be licensed in various ways, and may pass to heirs. In the event of infringement, a court may grant an injunction against the distribution of the offending invention and issue monetary damages to be paid to the patent holder. Short of legal recourse, the very existence of a patent in a certain field can scare away competing inventors.

The case of nanotechnology

Imagine if some firm held a patent on the brick. The patent would be drawn so broadly as to cover any "baked and/or glazed solid building element that would be used to construct lattice structures for human habitation." That firm would be able to charge royalties for most of the simple edifices in the world. It could designate which buildings would go up first and which would have to wait. There would probably be a rush to invent and patent a substitute for the patented brick that would be just different enough to preclude a lawsuit yet similar enough to work as easily and dependably as a brick. Some buildings would cost much more than they do now. Others might never get built at all. A tremendous amount of time and money would be spent trying to negotiate the brick-patent maze. Our world would certainly look different. As it stands, we are fortunate that we live in a world in which bricks are in the public domain. Anyone may make them, sell them, and use them to build their houses. Building—especially essential, low-cost building—may continue without concern for technological licenses and penalties.

But at a much smaller scale, we have allowed the brick to be patented. In the ill-defined world of "nanotechnology," a simple spheracule or rod of carbon—the "buckyball" or "nanotube" has been patented not once, but more than 250 times in slightly different forms. These items are to be the building blocks of more elaborate systems and technologies that are supposed to do work at sub-microscopic levels. The dream of nanotechnology— engineering substances at the scale of one nanometer (one billionth of a meter)—reveals many of the dangers of an overprotective patent system. Nanotechnology advocates predict that if the nanotechnology industry grows and thrives after significant research, these inventions could aid in health care, manufacturing, and computation by making many processes more precise and efficient. If predictions bear out, we should be able to control very small objects to deliver drugs into cells efficiently and effectively, thus limiting side effects. We should be able to repair all sorts of things from the molecular level up. Semiconductors and information-processing equipment should get smaller, lighter, cooler, and faster so that processing speed increases at a rate far beyond recent developments. And second-order nanotechnology should be able to generate "microbots," which would aid in fabrication and manufacturing with low energy inputs and remarkable purity and precision.

The patent system is supposed to generate a limited monopoly for a specific invention so that the patent holder may extract monopoly rents for a limited time. But by its very nature, nanotechnology complicates the assumptions that underlie the principles of patenting inventions. Nanotechnology bridges the conceptual gaps between substance and information, hardware and software, and technology and science. So it's a good place to examine the complexities and contradictions of the patent system.

Overall, the patent system seems to offer much to the nanotechnology industry. It offers instant global protection for inventions and processes years before they come to market— exactly the status of nanotechnology today. Tremendous potential remuneration exists for the firm or university that can exclude others from using an essential development in such a new area.

So being first matters. Patents work in such a way that coverage for a rather basic technology (such as nanotubes) can "reach through" to more complex uses of that technology, so that revenues could exponentially grow as other firms build on the original work downstream. The patent system is remarkably transparent. Filings are public and the knowledge inherent in the work can flow freely. Such knowledge might even be applicable to distinct work in other fields. In this way, patents work toward the public interest in ways quite distinct from trade secrets. And because patents expire in a reasonable amount of time, currently twenty years, the public domain is enriched constantly. And as key patents near expiration, firms that depend on those revenue streams push to improve or invent new things and methods. So if the patent system fit the technology and research demands, things could move quite nicely and many would benefit from the work. But do they fit?

As an emerging technology blessed with big expectations and small results so far, nanotechnology serves as an ideal case study to use to measure whether the U.S. patent system is working as it was intended, namely to foster widespread innovation and the free flow of information. The unique attributes and opportunities of nanotechnology promise to expose—and perhaps explode—the problems with the U.S. patent system. The question is: How should we change the patent system to foster both innovation and competition in nanotechnology so that as many people as possible may benefit from the inventions?

Despite the current claims that nanotechnology is more relevant to science fiction than science, billions of dollars have gone to firms—all of which hope against hope that they will be among first-movers in this field and marshal the great portion of what some claim will be a "$1 trillion prize." Many billions of investment dollars have come from states such as Singapore, Japan, the United Kingdom, and the United States. Yet billions more are destined soon to come from private-sector investors such as venture capital firms. But without any real products or processes to demonstrate yet, the only way a particular firm can assert itself as a leader in the field and generate sufficient confidence among investors for an invention that does not exist is to mark off as much intellectual territory as possible. This is even more important for small firms than large, established ones. As a result, we have witnessed a mini-industry of patent lawyers offering advice on how nanotechnology firms can "negotiate" the established patent terrain and generate effective "intellectual property strategies" that comprise various methods of filing for and enforcing patents, maintaining trade secrets, and protecting trademarks and copyrights as well.

By patenting the building blocks of nanotechnology before any of the more complex and useful structures come to market, nanotechnology companies are effectively blocking each other. They have formed a "patent thicket," requiring significant legal research, negotiation, and rights clearance before any second-level invention can occur without fear of a lawsuit. The rush to patent nanotubes and other basic elements has made further research and development risky and expensive.

Unlike other cutting-edge technologies, such as microprocessor-based computers, software, and biotechnology, the earliest discoveries and inventions of nanotechnology are occurring in an era of an overburdened patent system. These other areas of research and development were able to proceed without the cost and stress that competing patent claims put on a new industry. Beginning in the 1980s (but taking off during the 1990s) universities and firms went on a patent binge while the U.S. Patent and Trademark Office and the court that governs patents lowered the standards for patenting, allowing many more patents to be approved with less scrutiny. As a result, nanotechnology is endeavoring to start up at a time when knowledge flows less freely than it did during the software revolution.

The anti-commons

The patent mania of the late twentieth and early twenty-first centuries has created a "tragedy of the anti-commons" in various fields. A "commons" is a publicly owned resource. And publicly owned resources can be subject to overuse by many people, none of whom have a personal stake in preservation or rational use. The "tragedy of the commons," as ecologist Garrett Hardin described it in an influential 1968 paper, is best exemplified by a pasture used by multiple shepherds and their many sheep. Without state management or individual ownership, the sheep will graze until they kill all the grass, resulting in a loss for all. The tragedy is one of resource mismanagement. We all lose. A tragedy of the anti-commons is one in which too many essential items are owned by individuals so that search costs and transaction costs are high. People do not use resources optimally or boldly because it is too much trouble, too risky, or too expensive to do so. A tangle or "thicket" of patents covering small elements of a complex system can cause such a tragedy. In nanotechnology specifically, firms are pushed to claim the broadest possible patent protection as early as possible out of fear that some other firm or university will do it instead. As a result, recent years have witnessed an astounding surge of nanotechnology-related patents.

From 1997 through 2002, the number of U.S. patents issued that concerned nanotechnology in some way grew from 3,623 to 6,425. The most ambitious and authoritative study of the growth of nanotechnology patents has claimed that a broad, comprehensive search of patent databases has yielded more than 89,000 patents worldwide since 1976. The leading patenting nations are the United States (with more than 56,000), Japan (more than 7,500), France (more than 2,000), the United Kingdom (more than 870), Switzerland (more than 410), Taiwan (more than 380), Italy (more than 370), South Korea (more than 360), the Netherlands (more than 300), and Australia (more than 300). This list is not likely to change significantly in the next few years, and no state is likely to pass the United States in the number of nanotechnology patents issued. The fastest growing subgenres of nanotechnology patents are in the chemical and pharmaceutical fields. Semiconductor research follows closely behind.

A case can be made that early nanotechnology research could and should proceed without the protection, taxation, and consternation of the patent system. After all, right now nanotechnology is more science than technology (some would argue more science fiction than science). Basic research is supposed to be exempt from the patent system so that general knowledge (often paid for by state funding) can spread widely, be subject to scrutiny, and be able to serve to enrich more than one firm or inventor. Basic knowledge and discoveries are not supposed to be patentable; rather, they are meant to be open to all and subject to scientific scrutiny and fervent debate. In the absence of patent restrictions (and the temptation of massive rewards for exploiting knowledge), scientists could work for the pure satisfaction of discovery. They could act selfishly within an altruistic system, benefiting from higher cultural capital when they succeed. There might be less hype and more healthy skepticism—more science and less science fiction—if the patent system were kept at some length from basic research. The ethics of science would lead the frenetic demands of technology and commerce.

Perhaps the strongest argument for keeping the patent system away from basic research is that the public has already paid for it once. The governments of the world are pouring billions of dollars into basic research conducted by universities (many of them public), only to ensure that the beneficiaries of these grants will be able to tax the rest of us once again by bringing this work to market. Of the ten most important nanotechnology patents issued (as determined by the trade journal *Nanotechnology Law & Business*), seven are owned by major research universities in the United States: Northwestern University, the University of

California, Stanford University (two top-ten patents), Harvard University, the Massachusetts Institute of Technology, and the California Institute of Technology. The patent system has the potential to corrupt not only the process of basic research, but also the entire academic system. Since 1982 universities in the United States have been encouraged to exploit the basic research of their faculties to generate revenue from downstream commercial application. This development has generated a new set of incentives within the academy that favor commercially viable research over more speculative or esoteric research.

Imagine a world without patents

In June 2014 Elon Musk surprised his investors and most of the technology world. He posted on the Tesla Motors blog a statement that "Tesla will not initiate patent lawsuits against anyone who, in good faith, wants to use our technology." Tesla is one of the world's leaders in the production of automobiles that do not directly use fossil fuels. Musk, the founder and chief operating officer of Tesla, started the company in 2003. In the course of ten years Tesla invented and patented a slew of technologies, which, in helping to make its expensive, high-performance vehicles, have made Tesla a proof-of-concept for electric cars. Tesla finally sold enough cars to turn a profit in 2013. Several other companies, including Chevrolet, Ford, Toyota, and Nissan, had marketed less expensive electric cars available in select markets. But the technologies had not become standardized and the marginal cost of producing electric cars had not dropped significantly in the decade before. Musk explained in his blog post that Tesla had vigilantly defended its patents out of fear that larger companies would ride for free on Tesla's research and mass produce electric cars, rendering Tesla a historical footnote in the transformation of the world's energy use story. That's not what happened. Musk concluded that his patent portfolio had merely impeded technological progress and adoption by preventing meaningful competition. "We believe that Tesla, other companies making electric cars, and the world would all benefit from a common, rapidly-evolving technology platform," Musk wrote. "Technology leadership is not defined by patents, which history has repeatedly shown to be small protection indeed against a determined competitor, but rather by the ability of a company to attract and motivate the world's most talented engineers."

It is important to note that Musk did not proclaim that the patents would be in the public domain, and thus unenforceable. Tesla patents are still valid and potentially powerful. He merely promised not to sue another car company that used Tesla's technological designs "in good faith." It is unclear what "good faith" means. Tesla had not, as of the summer of 2016, outlined how it would make its patents "open source." All patents are by their very nature "open." To receive a patent one must disclose the nature and design of the technology and have it included in the database of a country's patent office. That is the essence of the public trade-off that justifies the state granting a patent. The rest of us may learn from the work and science that went into the invention, but the patent holder has a twenty-year monopoly on the commercial exploitation of that particular technology. Meanwhile, competitors may build upon the knowledge that informed the patented technology. And the patent holder may create a market to license the invention to other firms that could use it in more complex products and devices.

Overall, Musk's announcement seems very shrewd and one that is completely in the interest of his company. If Musk can encourage more automobile manufacturers to develop more long-range electric cars with mass appeal, then an incentive will exist for countries around the world to develop the charging and repair infrastructure that Tesla desperately needs to move beyond a niche market largely centered in California. If every service station in Europe and the United States saw potential revenue in charging stations and repair technicians to serve a standardized set of electric vehicles, then the world could move away from the internal-combustion, petroleum-product engine to something much more clean and efficient. And Tesla could become the Toyota of the twenty-first century.

Tesla was not the first car company to make such a move in the interest of industry standardization and the public good. In the late 1950s Volvo patented the three-point safety belt, and the firm urged other companies to adopt it instead of the less effective two-point lap belt. It took more than two decades for regulators around the world to push the rest of the automobile world to adopt the three-point belt as the standard. In the meantime, Volvo gained much more in terms of its reputation for making safe cars than it would have gained suing other car companies whose aim was to save a few lives. In both cases, the trademark and the reputation of the firm matter more than the defensive value of the patents. In Tesla's example it means more because the world must install an expensive new infrastructure to make electric cars as viable as diesel or gasoline cars. Volvo became a major global car company on the back of its reputation for protecting individual human bodies. Tesla could do the same by building a reputation for protecting the polar ice caps and the coral reefs of the world.

So why have patents at all? If Musk concluded that Tesla's patents were more trouble than they were worth and served only to hold his industry and company back, why don't more company leaders reach the same conclusion? And why shouldn't we all conclude that patents are an unnecessary drag on economic transactions and technological progress and so we should dismantle the patent system around the world?

Two economists working for the U.S. Federal Reserve Bank, Michele Boldrin and David Levine, published a paper in 2012 making the case that no empirical evidence exists that patents promote innovation in most industries. "There is strong evidence, instead, that patents have many negative consequences," they wrote. Great swells of innovation within and among new industries occur within legal and cultural environments that value competition and cooperation with relatively free flows of basic information. Patents are anticompetitive, Boldrin and Levine argued. Beyond mere nihilism, however, Boldrin and Levine allow that "weak patent systems may mildly increase innovation" and that a strong and broad consensus exists that the pharmaceutical industry successfully relies on patent protection to generate incentives and rewards that constantly push new medicines onto markets. But overall and on balance, they conclude that going without a patent system and instead relying on ensuring competitive markets and seeding research and development with competitive grants and prizes to address societal needs such as illness would be successful at encouraging innovation. And such practices would not create the "many negative side-effects" that are generated by the patent system.

The patent system works worst, Boldrin and Levine argue, in markets for complex computer hardware and software. In these cases, devices such as smartphones and tablets are made of hundreds of complex components with distinct lineages. Some of these technologies, such as global positioning system chips, emerged from government research. Others, such as the code for the touch-screen interface, came from a variety of large and small hardware and software makers during the course of almost twenty years. The "thicket" of overlapping and sometimes vaguely described patents that feed into a single device in your pocket is very expensive to navigate. It is impossible to imagine a small, independent creator designing and launching a better smartphone now. That company would need a vast team of patent lawyers, a multiyear time frame, and a big pool of cash to license the hundreds of patents from competing companies—all of which have an interest in quashing competition. That is one reason that we rarely see sophisticated devices emerging from companies not named Samsung, Nokia, or Apple. The transaction costs of clearing or defending a company against charges of infringing are high. Therefore the barriers to entering the market are also high.

Patent thickets

One acutely pernicious form of the anti-commons problem is a "patent thicket"—overlapping patents that cover the same product or process. The best-documented thicket concerns semiconductors. Semiconductor producers potentially infringe on hundreds of different patents owned by companies that harvest only patents. These firms produce no innovation. They merely seek rents from others who hope to bring technologies to market, thus profiting mightily from the patent arms race. When information is incomplete, as within an industry that is inherently multidisciplinary and requires searches for patents in a variety of areas, the dangers of patent thickets become even more pronounced.

The classic historical case of a "patent thicket" inhibiting innovation rather than encouraging it is the early U.S. airplane industry. Americans often boast of the success that Wilbur and Orville Wright enjoyed building and flying a powered aircraft at Kitty Hawk, North Carolina, in 1903. Alas, their legacy did more to impede the development of an American aircraft industry than spark it. That is because they ruthlessly defended their suspect patent over the method they used to control the aircraft. It is also because the Wrights made very bad aircraft. Other companies controlled other technologies that were essential to safe and effective mechanized flight. So while the patent held by the Wrights might have been the thorniest branch of the thicket, it was not the only one. The Wrights were so aggressive and successful at stopping other entrants into aviation that U.S. military officials feared the patent conflicts would prevent the United States from developing a strong military aircraft industry. By the time the United States entered World War I in 1917, U.S. Assistant Navy Secretary Franklin D. Roosevelt and others had pressured the Wrights to join a patent pool so that all the American aviation companies could use the patents of each of the companies without fear. The state-created patent pool succeeded.

And between World War I and World War II the United States was able to foster a creative and successful commercial and military aircraft industry.

It's not a hard case to make: For complex products like smartphones, tablets, high-definition "smart" televisions, robots, biotechnologies, airplanes, and automobiles—especially electric automobiles—patent thickets are a big drag on competition and innovation. Perhaps the state should step in to make it harder to get a patent. Perhaps some patents in some industries should be weaker and last far less than twenty years. Perhaps the state should use antitrust or competition policy to break up patent thickets when they are abusive and retard innovation. Perhaps we should scrap the patent system for most if not all industries in most if not all countries. Perhaps not.

Justifying patents

Sometimes government action is not needed. A notable patent thicket from the nineteenth century ended up resolving itself once the interested parties realized it was in their best interest to relax enforcement of their patents. No single person or company invented the sewing machine. Like most complex machines it is a combination of many different inventions. Several people and companies, including Elias Howe and Isaac Singer, contributed small and incremental advances to the development of a machine that people had long desired. Would-be inventors nurtured the dream of the sewing machine for nearly a century before the first sewing machine became commercially available as cotton from British colonies became cheaper and new markets for mass-produced goods emerged in the wake of rapid urbanization and industrialization. Harvesting, shipping, and processing cotton into threads, and weaving it into fabric had all become cheaply mechanized. The bottleneck to the mass production of clothing, tents, and sails remained sewing. The first patent related to the sewing machine was filed in 1755 in

Britain, but it did not yield a marketable product. Many other elements of the ultimate machine were patented in Germany, Austria, France, Britain, and the United States through 1850. Each small advance and its patent revealed a technological insight that could be borrowed without fear by inventors in other countries. No international agreement was in place to respect the patents of other countries. So both technology and knowledge flowed freely.

Howe was an early example of what we now call a "patent troll," someone who accumulates a series of patents for the purpose of shaking down other firms for license payments and judgments. Unlike many more recent trolls, Howe did contribute several important inventions and owned the patents for his own inventions. But he was not in the business of actually selling machines. Several other inventors in the 1840s came up with changes and improvements until Isaac Singer patented the last few changes in 1846 and prepared to market a real, working sewing machine. Several other companies also were selling sewing machines by the late 1840s. Because so many firms and people owned so many overlapping and complementary patents, it was impossible to cleanly produce an excellent sewing machine without either spending time and money licensing patents or just infringing dozens of them. The ensuing barrage of lawsuits among Howe, Singer, and several other inventors sparked what was known as the "Sewing Machine War" between 1849 and 1856. After much expense and exhaustion the major patent holders agreed to create the first American "patent pool," the Sewing Machine Combination. The four major companies in the pool agreed to compete in the sewing machine market but issued licenses for all their relevant patents, ensuring there would be no lawsuits or other transaction costs. The inventors received royalties. The firms were able to continue improving their products. Clothing, flags, sails, and tents became more plentiful and cheaper just in time for the U.S. Civil War.

4. An 1849 patent model of the first commercially successful sewing machine, invented by Isaac Singer. Singer built the first sewing machine with vertical needle movement powered by foot treadle. The sewing machine was the subject of one of the most important patent battles of the nineteenth century.

This historical antecedent serves as a cautionary tale for those who look at the patent mess between Samsung and Apple over the design and workings of their smartphones. Since 2011 Samsung and Apple have been fighting each other in courts in the United States, the United Kingdom, Germany, South Korea, and Japan over accusations that each company had infringed on the patents of the other for mobile smart telephones. In one of the most notorious decisions, Apple successfully sought a judgment against Samsung for violating its design patent covering a rectangular device with rounded corners:

the standard shape of any useful and comfortable phone. The court ruled, contrary to common sense, that rectangles are not "obvious" shapes for phones and that despite many phones before the IPhone that have borne rectangular shapes with rounded corners, there was no "prior art" that would invalidate Apple's patent. Every standard smartphone with a touch screen operates through dozens of patents that are owned by dozens of companies. Each major phone manufacturer and software provider, including Apple, Google, Samsung, and Microsoft, have been buying up bundles of patents and sometime whole companies (Motorola Mobile by Google; Nokia by Microsoft) to acquire their patents to smooth the process of phone development and to give them leverage against competitors.

The smartphone market is hampered by a classic patent thicket, much like the sewing machine market was in the 1850s. Should we just relax and let these suits settle out, despite the premium consumers must pay and the wasted money thrown at lawyers over litigation and negotiation because we trust that—like the sewing machine companies—these companies come to their senses and voluntarily form a patent pool? Or should we, as with the airplane, invite the strong arm of the state (or multiple states) to force a truce and forge a pool that would allow for these and newer companies to build upon the current state of the industry cheaply and boldly?

History offers us only anecdotal answers to these questions. The great patent debates of the 2000s have been guided as much by ideology as by evidence. Sadly, economists, lawyers, and policy professionals can't offer us solid empirical data favoring one set of patent policies over another. So instead the world's patent policies are a messy tapestry that reflect the powers of particular industries within different countries.

The case of pharmaceuticals

The pharmaceutical industry is the one field in which there seems to be consensus within research and development that patents are important, if not essential. It is difficult to imagine an effective and efficient pharmaceutical system that would work without a large number of private firms doing research on all sorts of remedies. The pharmaceutical system must be considered to include more than the classic firms like Merck and Bayer AG. It also includes biotechnology firms like AmGen and Genentech. And it includes hundreds of major research universities around the world that engage in both basic and applied research on diseases, their causes, and their treatments. Such a diverse and global set of actors can address the needs of potential consumers (or, rather, patients) as needs and demands change over time. They can use the surpluses earned from "blockbuster" drugs like Viagra or Zoloft to fund research on less potentially lucrative treatments for more obscure conditions. They can shift resources fairly gracefully as needs arise, competition mounts, and new technologies arrive. While much of the basic health and biological research that informs successful treatments starts with state funding through public universities, pharmaceutical companies have for more than a century succeeded rather impressively in bringing those treatments to market by relying on the temporary monopoly of twenty years of patent protection.

Even Boldrin and Levine concede in their nihilistic article that patents play an important role in encouraging innovation in the pharmaceutical industry. They credit the high value of the basic science disclosed in every patent application and published clinical trials. The public—through better research in which competing companies and universities may avoid repeating the mistakes of others and may build on the new knowledge revealed by others—benefits greatly through the continuing production of new drugs to tackle a wide array of ailments. Such privatized innovation with true competition limited by the power and duration of patents keeps prices of essential, life-saving drugs very high in most parts of the world. Antiretroviral drugs to treat AIDS, for instance, have been prohibitively expensive in much of the world since their debut in the 1990s. Great "welfare loss," as economists call it, occurs when strong patents on pharmaceuticals drive up the cost of staying healthy or staying alive in developing nations. One economic study predicted the cost of introducing patents in India to cover the Quinolones family of synthetic, broad-spectrum antibacterial drugs would be US$300 million, while the monetary benefit to the companies that produce these drugs would be less than US$20 million. These welfare losses include lost workdays, long-term medical costs, and the cost of dealing with a potential public health crisis if severe infections become pandemics. So on balance the development of pharmaceuticals could prove to be better without our current patent system, if not by scrapping patents altogether. Instead, Boldrin and Levine argue, we should enhance the role of and increase funding for state agencies that fund health and science research such that any research funded by the public may not result in privatized, patented remedies. Patents should be granted only when the applicant can demonstrate that they would not hurt competition. In other words, the burden of showing economic benefit should be on the patent applicant.

Overall, it is clear that the patent system does not provide enough inventive for pharmaceutical companies to research and bring to market all the life-saving or life-enhancing drugs that we need. The industry has not created any new antibiotics since the 1980s. Companies continue to press for "blockbuster" drugs that can treat widespread maladies that affect populations in the wealthier parts of the world. Such afflictions include baldness, impotence, and depression. In addition, companies increasingly invest in highly specialized, "personalized" treatments that help small numbers of patients yet can generate very high price tags. So a movement is growing to urge states to take greater control of the research and development decisions over new pharmaceuticals to better match the actual health needs of the world's populations. The patent system alone does not seem to be able to generate the right kinds of incentives.

Patenting life

No aspect of patent law generates more controversy than the fact that aspects of biology may be patented. The fact that in many places in the world some types of naturally occurring biological phenomena can be patented raises many thorny ethical questions. Should any aspect of human life be claimed and put on a market? Should the harvester of genetic material have greater rights over the use of and rewards from genetic material than the donor of that material? And what if a company makes the use of a gene prohibitively expensive for many people around the world?

Generally patents are not supposed to cover naturally occurring phenomena, only the improvements one adds to the effects of the natural phenomenon. One cannot patent the effects of gravity, for instance. But one could patent a new and better way to use gravity's pull on water to create electric power more efficiently. In the case of genes, the debate has been about whether the mere isolation of genes or sequences of genes constitutes an improvement on a natural phenomenon.

Since 1997 a company called Myriad Genetics has held patents around the world on gene sequences called BRCA1 and BRCA2. This gene is an important marker in the propensity to develop breast and ovarian cancers. A number of scientists had isolated the natural gene sequence as well as generated in a lab the complementary, or cDNA sequences. The patents covered both the "genomic," or natural, DNA and the cDNA. Myriad Genetics developed and sold a simple test that would tell patients whether they carried the sequence and thus could assess the likelihood of developing cancers. Because of the patent, no other company could develop such a test and no hospital could run such a test without paying license fees to Myriad. The test often cost patients or their insurers as much as US$3,000. This amount of money was beyond the reach of many.

Through a series of court challenges around the world, Myriad's lawyers argued that its scientists had invented novel procedures for finding and isolating the genes and made clear decisions about where to sever the sequences. And, they argued, by removing BRCA1 and BRCA2 from the string of genes in the cell they had effectively created a sequence that did not exist before. Without Myriad scientists and their work, they argued, BRCA1 and BRCA2 would not exist in that form at all. Thus these procedures were as invented as any mousetrap.

This argument carried force for many years. In February 2013 a court in Australia ruled in favor of Myriad and retained the patent. But three months later the U.S. Supreme Court ruled that Myriad's patents on the genomic, naturally occurring but severed genes were not valid. They were products of nature, not human effort and invention. However, the Court also ruled that the cDNA versions of the genes could be patented because they were created by human hands.

The struggle to define just which phenomena are "natural" and which are not continues in various fields. Pharmaceutical companies have been extracting and isolating the active ingredient from the hoodia plant, which grows in South Africa and Namibia. Those who have eaten the fruit of the plant have reported that it retards appetite and can aid in weight loss. But no studies have been conducted that come to that conclusion. And the plant in its natural state offers no windfall to pharmaceutical companies. Investing millions of dollars in developing a stable, effective, and portable distillation of its active ingredients offers the potential to exclude competitors. So far, that effort has failed. However, those who have grown and used hoodia for centuries see their discovery at risk. If a pharmaceutical company succeeds in producing an effective drug from the plant, the company will enjoy the windfall. The communities that brought the plant to the world's attention will get nothing. This phenomenon is called "biopiracy." And it is a common complaint in places rich in vegetative diversity and ancient healing traditions such as Brazil and India.

Business methods and non-obviousness

Other patent controversies have arisen of late over the concept of non-obviousness. A patent must cover not only the work of human minds and hands; it also must not perform a task in a way that would be obvious to anyone already working in that field. This standard has not been met with much rigor of late. Valid patents in the United States cover a method for swinging on a playground swing and another for a peanut-butter-and-jelly sandwich. The most notorious of these, however, is the "one-click" patent held by Amazon.com: "A method and system for placing a purchase order via a communication network." Just before Christmas 1999 Amazon requested and was granted an injunction against its chief competitor in online book sales, BarnesandNoble.com, which had been allowing customers to purchase books and charge them to a stored credit card with only one click of a computer mouse.

Such "business method" patents and those that cover basic functions of computer software and Web interfaces have proliferated in recent years. But it is important to note that the early boom in computer and software innovation between 1975 and 1995 occurred almost without patents. Only since about 1995 have firms sought patent protection for things such as methods of purchase. But there has been some pushback against this. In 2011 a European court invalidated Amazon's one-click patent and determined that it lacked the essential inventiveness required in Europe for patents. And the U.S. Supreme Court issued several decisions between 2010 and 2014 that have limited the scope of "business method" patents and that demand higher standards of inventiveness than the United States has operated with recently. Despite much criticism and these recent rulings, Amazon retains the one-click patent in the United States.

Globalizing patents

We already know what a patent-less system might look like.
The former Soviet Union had a nominal patent system during
its seventy-four-year history. But few Soviet citizens filed for
Western-style patent protection. Instead, inventors would receive
certificates of appreciation from the state and a cash reward. The
state took ownership of the invention. In the Soviet system all
decisions about research, development, product release, and
technological experimentation were directed centrally by the state.
This did not mean that nothing was developed in the Soviet
Union. Certain areas of knowledge, specifically theoretical physics,
mathematics, and what became known as "cybernetics" thrived
with significant state support. And, of course, the Soviet system
created many new weapons of war, including the notorious AK-47
rifle. But one could not judge an exclusively state-driven system
of research and development a success. It is easy for a weapons
engineer to get the support he needs under such a system. But no
tolerance is given for those who dream big technological dreams.
We did not see innovations as influential as television, effective
pesticides, or vaccines emerge from Soviet labs. They did keep
pace in large technological systems such as space exploration,
largely because market actors were incapable of pursuing such
dreams anyway. Space programs had to be state driven. Then, in
1991, with the dissolution of the Soviet Union on the horizon
and a new spirit of "glasnost," or "openness," flowing through
society, the Soviet government adopted a more European-style
patent system in an effort to integrate with the larger global
economy. The new post-Soviet republics soon adopted similar
systems after the breakup.

A hybrid technological ecosystem, such as the ones that exists in most
of Europe and North America, seems to work fairly well. The state
can direct resources toward basic research that has no immediate
use. It also can foster technologies that have potential military uses,
such as the Internet or global positioning systems, and later release

them for public use and development. And a state-supported patent system, properly constructed, can foster innovation without corrupting competition too much.

The world is a patchwork of such hybrid systems. Some states invest almost nothing in medical, science, or technology research. And some states have weaker patent systems than others. This scenario is changing quickly. Since the mid-1990s states have been compelled to standardize or "harmonize" their patent systems with the strongest systems in the world—those of the United States and western Europe—as part of the deal for joining the global flow of trade and technology. However, weak efforts toward harmonization are much older. In 1883 many industrializing states signed the International Convention for the Protection of Industrial Property. This treaty gave reciprocal patent rights among the signatory states. Since 1977 the entire European Community (present-day European Union) has shared a common patent office and process. By 1986, the Uruguay Round of the General Agreement on Tariffs and Trade (GATT) generated the Agreement on Trade-Related Aspects of Intellectual Property Rights (TRIPS). The TRIPS accord binds all nations that are members of the World Trade Organization (WTO) to respect the patents of each of the signatory states. The agreement has "harmonized" the patent process, setting minimal standards of protection.

Of course, this process of "harmonization" significantly undermines state sovereignty. Individual states may no longer tailor their patent systems for their particular industrial, public health, or development needs. One major improvement to this push for standardization came in 2001 when the World Trade Organization yielded to pressure from countries that had growing public health crises such as widespread HIV infections. Led by India and Brazil, these nations pushed for passage of what has come to be known as the Doha Declaration on TRIPS and Public Health. It ensured that member states could take necessary measures to protect public health, even if that meant failing to enforce pharmaceutical patents to the fullest. Countries now have the right to make cheaper versions of life-saving drugs when there is a national emergency. This provision was met with resistance from the United States, Switzerland, and other countries that host powerful pharmaceutical companies with expensive research portfolios. And the execution of this provision remains muddy. But lives have been saved because many can now acquire cheaper versions of patented medicines.

The consequences of too much faith in "innovation"

A Connecticut Yankee in King Arthur's Court does not end well for Hank Morgan or for Merlin, his nemesis. Morgan's inventions, his ideology, and his patent office could not save him in his war against the clerics and wizards. Ultimately, those who controlled the stories, the lessons, and the myths and legends triumphed—but at a cost of more than 30,000 lives lost to mines, electric fences, and machine guns. Twain leaves us shocked and dismayed about the costs of an unerring belief in "progress" for the sake of "progress." Although he never uses the twentieth-century term noted in this chapter that has dominated the discourse over patent law— "innovation"—Twain would certainly roll his weary eyes at the conflation of "innovation" and "progress." The U.S. Constitution empowers Congress to create a patent systems "to promote the progress" of the "useful arts." And "progress" is not a value-free concept. After more than two centuries of tinkering with the patent system and celebrating the tinkering in workshops, laboratories, and factories, we are no closer to fully understanding how the patent system "promotes progress." And thus the struggle to design an ideal patent system—one that creates just enough incentive to drive invention forward yet does not stifle markets nor drive up prices for important products—continues.

Chapter 4

Trademarks and the politics of branding

On a Saturday morning in early February 2014 a crowd began queuing outside a familiar looking new store in the Los Angeles neighborhood of Los Feliz. It had a green awning. Above the awning sat a green-and-white logo with a mermaid in the center of a circle. Around the circle letters spelled out "Dumb Starbucks Coffee." Inside bemused customers drank in the irony along with plenty of "Dumb Iced Caramel Mocha." They were offered compact discs of music labeled "Dumb Norah Jones" and "Dumb Jazz Standards." Customers were offered information about the store in the form of a "frequently asked questions" notice. "By adding the word 'dumb' we are technically 'making fun' of Starbucks, which allows us to use their trademarks under a law known as 'fair use,'" the flyer reads. "In the eyes of the law, our 'coffee shop' is actually an art gallery and the 'coffee' you're buying is considered the art." The mystery of why someone would do something so elaborate and, well, dumb compelled many to make inquiries in linking to stories about the store on Facebook and Twitter. News programs in Los Angeles and around the United States covered the mystery. The stunt did not last long. Los Angeles County health inspectors, not lawyers for the real Starbucks, shut down the shop after seventy-two hours.

The purveyor of "Dumb Starbucks" turned out to be a comedian named Nathan Fielder, host of an until-then unsuccessful television show called *Nathan for You*. He is a professional prankster. His usual shtick is to convince a wary small business owner to go along with one of his crazy schemes to improve their market share. Fielder boasts of having a degree in business administration and calls himself a consultant. The program skewers the language and satirizes the culture of business consultants as he reveals his character to be profoundly stubborn, confident, and—well—dumb. In the "Dumb Starbucks" episode, however, Fielder starts a business for himself. And it goes badly. Yet as parody, it succeeds. Fielder exposed the various ways that global companies like Starbucks rely on their trademarks and trade dress more than they do their actual products. Much of the episode is devoted to Fielder's efforts, on advice of his lawyer, to establish himself as a well-known parody artist so that Starbucks lawyers and future courts in which he might appear would easily distinguish his "art" experiment from any attempt to ride for free on the reputation of Starbucks. Fielder acts like a horrible parodist of trademark law but turns out to be a masterful parodist of parody.

Control of trademarks is control of language. Trademarks, whether they are images, logos, names, or phrases, are ubiquitous in most of the world. They are part of everyday life as much as are popular songs or powerful stories. They make up a significant set of the symbols through which we construct our identities, affiliations, and associations. But control of trademarks is also important to us as consumers. The driving justifications for trademarks have nothing to do with incentives. Unlike copyrights and patents, the world does not need more brands. Instead, consumer protection and convenience justify these restrictions on expression. As with many such restrictions, courts and legislators have punched some breathing holes in trademark protections. The right to claim "fair use" through parody is one such hole. It is an important one, even if the "Dumb Starbucks" stunt used it clumsily. But trademarks, like other forms of intellectual property, also regulate commercial competition. We cannot fully understand trademarks and their effects if we fail to consider the consequences with respect to culture, competition, and consumer protection of the work that trademarks do in the world.

I am writing this in a different Starbucks from the one in Charlottesville that I described earlier. This one is not obviously "dumb." There is no parody here. There is just the carefully engineered sincerity that Starbucks sells so well. This is just a regular Starbucks, much like any other Starbucks, thanks to the idea of "trade dress." This one is in Boston, Massachusetts. I'm typing on a laptop computer with a glowing Apple on it. I am sipping green tea from a decorated plastic cup with an identifiable green straw. I am wearing a navy blue shirt with the logo of both Nike (the ancient Greek goddess of victory) and Futbol Club Barcelona.

Just minutes ago I smiled and nodded at a ten-year-old boy in this Starbucks who was wearing an FC Barcelona jacket. Earlier in the

5. Camp Nou, home of Futbol Club Barcelona (also known as FC Barça), displays on its seats the trademarked slogan "Més que un club" (More than a club). FC Barça is one of the most financially successful sports franchises in the world and has a lucrative partnership with Nike.

day a man working in a dry cleaning shop struck a conversation with me about FC Barça's recent signing of serial biter Luis Suarez and the prospects of forward Neymar coming back from a serious back injury. On my way to the Starbucks I smiled and nodded to a man who—like me—dared to wear a New York Yankees cap in downtown Boston. The Yankees and FC Barça both use navy blue in their official uniforms. But they are different and very specific—and thus trademarked—hues of blue. FC Barça also incorporates the colors of the flag of Catalonia in its official crest.

The logos I wear on my journeys say things about me—perhaps not altogether positive things, depending on one's views of powerhouse sports franchises, global sweatshop purveyors, and sports-fan-based consumerism in general. Regardless of the overall messages I send when I dress like this, I am able to form quick bonds with others who share my affiliations. These are not deep connections. But they open me up to social engagement (and derision, in the case of my Yankee cap in Boston) that I might otherwise never enjoy. For this small pleasure I pay a premium to be able to display logos in which I have no financial investment. A navy knit cotton shirt without the FC Barça logo would cost less than half what I paid for this one. In any major city in North America or Europe—or just about anywhere else in the world, for that matter—it's highly likely that on any given day you will encounter a person bearing trademarked brands on their body, even if a substantial number of the products on which these marks sit are counterfeit. Within this global flow of words, sounds, images, coffee, food, and beer, trademarks operate as a central and pervasive regulatory mechanism. While the flow is global and almost universal, trademark law and its consequences are not.

The incomplete globalization of trademarks

Like patents, but unlike copyright, trademarks do not work within a global regulatory system. Companies that wish to exploit their trademarks in particular countries must register, use, and defend their marks within and among the various shades and differences of trademark law around the world. International treaties allow for standardized, multicountry registration. But differences abound, as the makers of Budweiser beer have discovered.

There are two distinct makers of Budweiser beer, it turns out. There is the American brand, Budweiser, owned by Anheuser-Busch InBev, a Brazilian-Belgian holding company based in Brussels that purchased the St. Louis food and beverage company in 2008. The company has long sought to make the watery, American-style Pilsner beer Budweiser a global brand. Anheuser-Busch InBev is the largest brewer in the world, and its various brands, including Beck's, Hoegaarden, Leffe, and Modelo, comprise 25 percent of the world's beer consumption. Budweiser won the bidding to be the official beer of the 2014 World Cup tournament in Brazil, and FIFA successfully lobbied to change Brazilian law to allow for beer to be sold in World Cup stadia.

Anheuser-Busch InBev's desire for global ubiquity for its flagship brand has been thwarted, however, by a smaller, newer brewing company in the Czech Republic. Budejovicky Budvar Brewery is a state-owned company in the town of České Budějovice. It was known as "Budweiss" when the Austro-Hungarian Empire ruled much of eastern Europe. It has been selling a Pilsner-style beer called "Budweiser" since about 1875—about the same time that Anheuser-Busch began selling its own "Budweiser" in the United States. In the past it was expensive and difficult to transport beer across a small country—let alone across the Atlantic. So most towns in Europe developed their own breweries and rarely traded across borders or bodies of water. During the Cold War, of course, few if any goods moved across the Iron Curtain. Since 1989, however, we have seen massive integration of food and beverage trade. This development has been facilitated by lower legal trade restrictions and tariffs, as negotiated through the World Trade Organization treaty process. It also has been enabled by improvements in shipping and storage technology.

So by the end of the twentieth century many formerly local brands of food and beverages were poised to find new consumers around the world. In 1994 Anheuser-Busch proposed an agreement that would divide the world's markets between the two companies. The Czech government rejected it and instead focused on defeating the then-American company by taking advantage of its established presence in the just evolving European Union. Since about 2000 the two companies have clashed in courtrooms around the world in each seeking to be the exclusive user of the trademark "Budweiser." Meanwhile, the Czech beer is marketed in the United States as "Czechvar." In 2011 the European Court of Justice ruled that Budejovicky Budvar has exclusive right to use "Budweiser" in the European Union. But enforcement locally has not been that simple. In France, one can ask for the American version by asking for a "Bud," which is another trademark that Anheuser-Busch InBev uses for the same product. In Germany, one may ask for "Anheuser-Busch B." A court in Portugal ruled in June 2014 that only the Czech product may be called "Budweiser." And in the United Kingdom, both the Czech and the American versions are legally allowed to use "Budweiser," so there is what one might call duel exclusivity—or no exclusivity at all, from Anheuser-Busch InBev.

To the Czech company, the conflict is about more than a trademark. It is about a cultural tradition of brewing and the appropriation by a multinational conglomerate of local designations (Pilsen is a Czech city as well). Geographic designations are related to trademarks, in the sense that they are supposed to indicate a form of authenticity that might help consumers understand the origin and style of their products or—at least—defend small, local cultural forms of production from large multinational conglomerates like Anheuser-Busch InBev. The global battles over trademark, trade dress, and local designations are part of a larger power struggle between the large and the small, the global and the local, and those who wish for language and symbols to flow freely with less thorny regulation and those who wish to protect traditional communities threatened by the torrent of globalized symbols.

What do trademarks do?

Trademarks allow a company to offer a consistent product or some predictable quality. For instance, whenever you buy a beverage labeled "Coca Cola," you assume from the name on the can that it will taste a certain way, and that it will taste just like the last Coke you drank. However, it's important to note that trademarks do nothing to guarantee a product's quality or consistency. Companies must have an investment in their long-term reputations for trademarks to perform their social functions. So while there is no patent-like incentive policy goal to create more trademarks, there is a policy justification in creating an incentive through the rising value of the mark for the company that owns it to consistently maintain quality goods and services. Of course, in a monopolistic or oligopolistic market companies need not care about quality goods or service and they still get to defend their trademarks.

The second major justification for trademarks is what economists call "search costs." Without clear, consistent, memorable, and legally protected marks to guide us, we would spend time, energy, and even money trying to find that beverage that tastes just like the one from last weekend. It is not clear how distracting or costly such searches would be without a legal monopoly on a logo or word. We manage to locate goods using generic terms like "aspirin" (an active trademark of Bayer AG until the 1919 Treaty of Versailles forced the German company to relinquish the mark in France, the United Kingdom, Russia, and the United States). Therefore, the social value of trademarks is minimal, but it is real. The commercial and proprietary value of trademarks is, however, enormous.

Those who use trademarks in their work—marketers and advertisers—don't consider consumer protection or "search costs"

6. The official Olympic flag waves at the Panathenaic Stadium in Athens. Since 1981, the International Olympic Committee has held exclusive rights over uses of the word "Olympics" and of the interlocking rings displayed on the flag. Many businesses around the world have been threatened with legal action for using the word "Olympic" in their names and displaying the Olympic symbol.

when they roll out new trademarks or defend their old ones. They consider a mark to be something established and earned—a proxy for the actual value that the company has worked for in the market. For them, trademarks are just their property. So understandably business leaders take an absolutist view of their use and against their abuse.

While, unlike patents and copyrights, trademarks may last indefinitely, a trademark owner must keep the mark active in commerce and must ensure that no one overuses the mark to signify competing products. Such overuse would erode the communicative value of the mark because people would start to disassociate the trademark from the company of origin. This happened most famously with Zipper, a term first used in 1923 by the B. F. Goodrich company to describe an interlocking-teeth clothing fastener. The invention had been patented in 1917 and so the patent expired in 1937. Goodrich licensed the patent for use on rubber boots. Because so many people soon regularly called such fasteners zippers, regardless of the origin of the term, Goodrich could not claim that it had been using the term exclusively. It is unclear whether Goodrich tried to secure a trademark on "Zipper," but it would have soon been impossible to do anyway. The mark had "gone generic" or had been "genericized." The legal test for a mark "going generic" is when it loses its "secondary meaning" among a significant number of consumers. This could be a general population or it could be a small group within a specialized industry. The fear of trademark erosion has motivated many companies to aggressively defend the use of their names in common speech and writing. For years Xerox would purchase advertisements in the *Columbia Journalism Review* to remind journalists that Xerox was not a verb meaning "to photocopy" and that not all photocopy machines were Xerox machines. The very success of Xerox threatened to undermine its ability to defend its trademark.

What trademarks don't do

One general principle of trademark law limits the exclusivity of the mark to the market in which the owner is operating. The test is supposed to be whether the use by the second company would cause confusion in the minds of consumers. This is why Delta Airlines and Delta Faucet may both use "Delta" in their respective areas of trade. No reasonable consumer is going to conflate those two products and services, and thus no reasonable consumer is going to conflate the companies either. They may both defend and enhance the value of their brand through exclusive use of "Delta."

However, this principle has been compromised in the United States in recent years by some revisions to the law that attempt to protect against "dilution." In the European Union and the United States a trademark can suffer dilution either by being blurred or by being tarnished. The blurring of a mark can occur when a vendor in a field or market beyond the core market of the trademark holder invokes a similar mark in such a way that it inflates the communicative power of the mark. A mark may be tarnished when the trademark is associated with a product or service that a court considers untoward, unwholesome, or potentially embarrassing to the trademark holder. To establish that a trademark has been tarnished or blurred, a court need not find that the second use is likely to cause confusion among customers. In other words, the basic test of common sense has been tossed out of trademark enforcement. The rise of dilution has significantly shifted the balance of trademark protection in favor of large, established companies with famous trademarks. In fact, the fame of the mark is one of the criteria necessary to establish if one wishes to pursue a case based on dilution.

Considering dilution is a strange process of subjective mind reading and projection. Courts consider the following: the degree of similarity between the two marks; the degree of inherent or acquired distinctiveness of the famous mark; the extent to which the owner of the famous mark is engaging in substantially exclusive use of the mark; the degree of recognition of the famous mark; whether the user of the mark or trade name intended to create an association with the famous mark; and any actual association between the mark or trade name and the famous mark. In other words, a court need only conclude that the famous mark could mean a little less in the public mind if the new product carried the same name or color scheme. The effects of a rise of dilution claims would have made a bigger difference in the practice of trademark enforcement except that it has grown so easy to claim the likelihood of confusion that American trademark holders have not found it necessary to make the specific dilution claim. So while the principle that trademarks work only within core markets is still part of the theory, and Delta Airlines and Delta Faucet coexist quite nicely without any harm to consumers or to the two businesses, in practice strong trademarks controlled by aggressive companies have the power to squelch all sorts of smaller businesses that attempt to use similar names and designs for very different businesses.

But not every claim of dilution succeeds. In 1994 a small, family-run coffee roaster in Center Tuftonboro, New Hampshire, introduced a blend of coffee called "Charbucks." The coffee house, Black Bear Micro Roastery, had no intention of muscling in on Starbucks's global markets. It merely wanted to make the undeniable point that Starbucks overroasts its coffee beans, rendering the taste more smoky than subtle. Starbucks sued, claiming that the use of a brand of roasted coffee that so easily evokes thoughts of Starbucks dilutes its own, more famous brand. After nine years of court battles, an appeals court ruled in 2013 that Charbucks does not infringe on Starbucks's trademarks. "Thus, although the term 'Charbucks' is similar to 'Starbucks' in sound and spelling when compared out of context, the marks are only minimally similar as they are presented in commerce," the court ruled. "Here, the Charbucks marks are used exclusively with terms 'Mister,' 'Mr.' or 'Blend' and in contexts dissimilar from the contexts in which the Starbucks marks are used." So, as it turns out, Nathan Fielder's "Dumb Starbucks" prank had more going for him than just a parody fair use defense.

Fair use and free speech

Courts often have ruled that stiff protection of trademarks would restrict artistic expression or critical speech about products. The Louis Vuitton trademark was not diluted by the use of the term "Chewy Vuitton" for a pet chew toy that was "evocative" of a Louis Vuitton bag. The defendant produced a line of chew toys that parodied famous designers such as "Furcedes" (parodying Mercedes) and Chewnel No. 5 (Chanel No. 5). The court determined that Chewy Vuitton was a parody and that a successful parody would not dilute the famous brand but, in fact, may make it even more famous. So the University of Alabama could raise a

7. A roadside stand near the ruins of Ephesus in Turkey offers "genuine fake watches" displaying many of the most popular trademarks for jewelry and fashion.

complaint about an artist who paints and sells works that bear the precise hue of crimson and cream that the university claims in its trademark registrations. In fact, the University of Alabama did just that. It filed suit against artist Daniel Moore for depicting moments from notable Alabama football games. In 2103 Moore prevailed in the suit brought by the university, arguing successfully that his free speech rights trumped the trademark claim.

How are trademarks different from patents and copyrights?

Unlike patents and copyrights, trademarks can last forever as long as they are in use and retain their meaning in markets and culture. This makes sense because they never stop performing their function—helping consumers find consistency and protecting the reputation of companies—as long as the products still circulate. Again, trademarks have very different philosophical justifications than patents and copyrights. We have patents to provide incentives to invent and bring to market new technologies. We have copyrights to provide incentives to creators to bring their works to market. Society does not need more trademarks. And the public bargains inherent in the copyright and patent systems do not exist for trademarks. Patents require public disclosure of the knowledge and techniques that make the invention possible. Copyright lets facts and ideas flow freely while protecting only specific expressions.

Companies have much incentive to try to double- or triple-wrap their products in layers of protection. We already have seen how music, video, and book vendors use digital rights management to double wrap copyrightable material. And much computer software have both copyrights (which expire long after the software ceases being useful) and patents (which require disclosure but control ideas). Many products such as pharmaceuticals enjoy patent protection and trademark protection so that once the patent expires and generic versions of the drug come on the market, the inventing company can retain the reputational advantage of being the first mover in the market. And we have seen that something as mundane as a Starbucks coffee cup sleeve can bear protection by patents, trademark, and (in previous incarnations) copyright. But there are limits to this sort of overprotection. Trademarks are not available for functional attributes to a product. So there is no trademark on the pattern of interlocking nubs on a Lego piece. Nor can there be trademark protection for the overall structural design of clothing, because clothing is functional. If trademarks were available for the design of functional attributes, then companies could double-protect their inventions. Once a patent expired, the trademark could render the design exclusive to the company indefinitely. This would undermine the public bargain inherent in patents. Fictional characters, however, are frequently double-wrapped by copyright and trademarks. The pioneer in this practice was Edgar Rice Burroughs, who secured a trademark on Tarzan in the 1920s. Because the original Tarzan stories are in the public domain now, anyone may write a story about the character. But only the heirs to Edgar Rice Burroughs may license the likeness and name of Tarzan for toys, lunch boxes, Halloween costumes, or loincloths.

As with any other right, increasing one party's power decreases another party's liberty. As trademarks have become more valuable as goods and services seek out larger and farther markets, they also have grown in power. As in the case of Dumb Starbucks and other pranks, there are occasional demonstrations of the limits of trademarks. The struggle to control or liberate these elements of daily life, these linguistic elements, is about expanding or limiting "semiotic democracy," namely the ability of any citizen, not just the wealthy and powerful, to make use of the elements of culture and language that surround us to comment on our conditions and forge new expressions. Copyright is a major front in the struggle for semiotic democracy. Trademarks are part of the same field. But they operate very differently and exist for very different reasons.

Chapter 5

Other rights: Domain names, publicity, trade secrets, data, and designs

The many other forms of intellectual property beyond the big three—copyright, patent, and trademark—reflect particular and national agendas and political power structures. Some of them exist only in particular countries. Others protect narrow interests. In some cases governments will create a new set of rights because a new technology or practice does not fit easily into any of the big three. Because these systems of rights are so different in theory and practice from copyright, patent, or trademark, they are often called sui generis, Latin for "of its own kind."

Domain names

Trademarks protect goods within a market and work only within specified borders. But what about the names of something ephemeral like a website, something that is not exactly for sale, although it could serve as the platform for commerce? In the world of commerce the likelihood that two people or companies with exactly the same name offering competing products within the borders of the same state is unlikely. And when such a thing occurs, the trademark holder who has been in that business the longest (while keeping the mark in play) generally prevails in court. Such conflicts do not usually even get to court because lawyers will steer their clients around such obvious conflict.

But when the World Wide Web began attracting the attention across the globe of both individuals, who sought to express themselves, and firms, which hoped to reach new markets, such conflicts were immediate, common, and fierce. Because no state's laws prevailed over others, no one was sure how concepts like "fair use" would operate. Should the name of a domain (the term we use for websites such as www.oup.com) belong to the party that first registered the domain or to the party that had been doing business under that title for many years?

In 1998 the U.S. Department of Commerce contracted with a new nongovernmental, standards-setting organization called the Internet Consortium of Assigned Names and Numbers (ICANN) to handle the process and write the rules of domain name governance and distribution. The U.S. government did not have the authority to make the determination that ICANN would have that power. But it did it nonetheless, and the rest of the world just went along with the decision because no one had a better idea at the time—or since. ICANN is governed by a volunteer board of sixteen members largely selected by "stakeholder" groups. Its governing laws and structure strive to work through consensus and with open debate among global interests.

One of ICANN's chief duties is to determine which sites are eligible to acquire domain names with particular suffixes, or "top-level domain names," such as .com, .edu, .uk, .de, or .org. Another of its core functions, and the one most pertinent to intellectual property, is its uniform dispute resolution policy (UDRP). When someone registers a domain name, she agrees to abide by any ruling that ICANN's UDRP issues. A party agrees not to pursue legal action in court. So ICANN effectively globally governs this one practice of Internet commerce. The UDRP rules were written in close collaboration with the World Intellectual Property Organization, so ICANN has been subject to criticism that the rules are tilted in favor of established trademark holders.

To prevail in a dispute, a complaining party must show that the other domain registrant does not have any other legal claim to the name, such as a trademark issued, and that the other registrant pursued the domain name in "bad faith." In addition, and most importantly, the complainant must show that the new domain name is strikingly similar to a registered trade mark or service mark. So if someone had moved early to register for "Madonna. com" before the entertainer did, the entertainer would have to show that the new registrant does not have a good reason for owning such a domain. Thus, if the new registrant actually were named "Madonna" it might count in her favor. But if the registration was just an attempt to extort a fee from the entertainer to transfer the domain or it was intended to fool the public into believing it is a representative site, then the UDRP would favor the entertainer. Such a dispute between Madonna and a man named Dan Parisi (not Madonna) actually occurred in 2000. And Madonna prevailed, as she tends to in all matters. This process is considerably quicker and less expensive than litigation would be, especially given the difficulty of pursuing judgments in so many different countries. So while trademark law serves as a foundation for control over a domain name, it is not exactly the same and has a very different process for the resolution of conflicts.

Geographic marks

No dominant firm in Parma, Italy, makes and sells Parmigiano cheese. No major international corporation is based in Champagne, France, that endeavors to stock that region's sparkling wines in bars and restaurants around the world. Yet cheesemakers in Parma and winemakers in Champagne collectively have rights that they exercise over the use of "Parmigiano" and "Champagne" in their respective markets. These are not trademarks. They are not tied to a particular brand or company. They represent the work of a region. Since the early twentieth century, France has protected regions from which cheese, wine, truffles, and other foods originate through a system called *appellation d'origine contrôlée* (AOC). With the establishment of the European Union in the 1990s, all of Europe now issues strong protections to regional sources of both agricultural and processed products such as beer. The relationship between geographic indicators and trademarks is weak, although the justification is similar. Consumers should not be fooled into purchasing cheese from Wisconsin that looks like it comes from Switzerland, especially if they are paying a premium for a luxury good. And just as—if not more—importantly, the farmers, cheesemakers, and wine producers around the world who produce their goods with traditional methods should be protected from the economies of scale and political power of large multinational food conglomerates like Kraft or Anheuser-Busch InBev. In India geographic indicators have been applied to protect growers of products such as Basmati rice (as opposed to Texmati brand rice from Texas) or the leaves of the Neem tree, which is alleged to have many healing properties. So geographic indictor protection serves both as trade protection (and thus works against the general trend toward greater global integration of markets) and as cultural policy, preserving something of the traditions of local craft and foodways.

Of course, like trademarks, geographic indicators can "go generic." So while "Parmigiano" enjoys protection, "parmesan" long ago became associated with the stale, flavorless flakes of the cheese product that Kraft encases in plastic tubes. Thus "parmesan" is generic and cheesemakers in Parma have no control over its distribution. And if a trademark application comes too close to resembling a registered geographic indicator in Europe, then the registration will be denied.

In the United States, which does not have a strong tradition or sui generis protection of geographic origins, traditional trademarks often work on behalf of onions from Vidalia, Georgia, or oranges from Florida. Alas, Buffalo, New York, has not yet asserted its claims on "Buffalo wings." The United States, as a signatory state

8. A display of Italian cheeses at Mercato Centrale in Florence. European law protects the use of Protected Designations of Origin (PDO), which describe the sources of cheeses and prevent manufacturers from other places from selling cheese with those local designations—for example, pecorino Crotonese from the town of Crotone in southern Italy.

to the Trade-Related Aspects of Intellectual Property Rights (TRIPs) treaty, is obligated to protect other countries' geographic indicators if another product causes confusion in the marketplace and falsely represents its origin. But the United States still has a much less developed tradition of enforcing geographic indications, largely because it does not have a tradition of respecting *terroir*, or the "sense of place" that many who produce wine and cheese assert exists in a discernible form when a product comes from a place with a distinctive soil or, in the case of cheese, bacteria.

Personality rights

Individual people also have a property right that lies beyond the contours of trademark. In many places in the world, individuals have a "right of publicity" or a "personality right" that limits how others may exploit their names and images for commercial purposes. Usually these rights have limitations that allow for news organizations to use images of individuals. Rights of publicity emanate from privacy and trespass law, not classic intellectual property theory. The idea behind them is that people should have some control over how they are portrayed in the commercial mediascape. But one justification parallel with trademark is the idea that the public should not be fooled into believing that a celebrity has endorsed a commercial product when she has not. Of course, just as importantly, the celebrity who might want to venture into the market of commercial endorsement should be able to do so without risk of having her image appropriated for nothing and applied to products in which she does not believe and that has not been paid to endorse.

Canada, Denmark, France, Germany, China, and many other countries have varieties of personality rights. In the United States such laws are called rights of publicity and are not a function of federal law. These rights in the United States depend on state laws and case law. As of 2014, twenty-eight of the fifty United States had specific rights of publicity statutes, with California and New York hosting the bulk of cases (unsurprisingly, as celebrities and media organizations tend to cluster in those states). Indiana, for some reason, has the strongest celebrity protection laws. Rights to publicity laws in the United States are curbed significantly by the first amendment of the U.S. Constitution, which guarantees free speech and a free press. There is some debate over the need for a right to publicity because unfair competition tort law should and does protect individuals from having their celebrity appropriated for false endorsements. Nonetheless, the cultural and commercial power of celebrity has served to double-protect its own interests.

9. A woman riding the subway in New York City wears tights
displaying multiple faces of actor Ryan Gosling. Celebrities in the
United States enjoy a "right of publicity" that allows them to sell and
control the rights to the use of their names, faces, and likenesses on
commercial goods. Sometimes, however, manufacturers use their
likenesses without permission.

Trade secrets

The best example of a successfully protected trade secret is the recipe for Coca-Cola. If the company had patented it back in the late nineteenth century, the formula long ago would have lapsed into the public domain and dozens of companies could use the formula disclosed in the patent application to make an identical beverage. By keeping the information secret, Coca-Cola retains complete control for as long as it wants.

Unlike federal patent and copyright laws, trade secret laws are extended and enforced through the common law. It is extra-legislative in origin, yet it is a powerful part of "intellectual property." Since 1979, forty-seven states in the United States have passed a law called the Uniform Trade Secrets Act, standardizing the definition, terms, and punishments for violating trade secrets. Trade secret laws are common throughout the world, and the Trade-Related Aspects of Intellectual Property Rights treaty sets out minimal standards for member nations to protect. As with U.S. law, the basic standards are that the information must be secret, it must have commercial value, and it must have been subject to reasonable steps to keep it secret.

An idea's perceived economic value is the chief basis for a trade secret. But to enforce it and punish those who release secrets, the firm must show that it took some measures to keep the information secret. These measures might include locking the secrets in a safe, encrypting digital documents, or restricting circulation of the information to a particular stratum of management on a "need-to-know" basis. Unlike patents, trade secrets theoretically could last forever. That is one of the reasons so many companies, such as Coca-Cola, rely on secrets rather than patents. Trade secrets are violated through larceny, spying, or bribery. If a secret is made public, it cannot be considered secret once again. Often employees will be required to sign nondisclosure agreements that contractually bind the employee over and above trade secret law and often limit the employee's ability to find work with competing firms in the same markets.

Misappropriation and data protection

When one company takes the secrets of another, it faces civil action under trade secret law. But what if a company takes information that another company has assembled and made publicly available? There might be commercial value to this information. And compiling the information certainly cost time, money, and effort. But copyright does not protect facts or data. It protects only the creative modes of expression of those facts or data. And copyright has never been designed to reward labor or investment.

Courts in the United States have developed a tort called "misappropriation" to handle such situations. During World War I the Associated Press news service employed reporters around the world to write reports and send them to newspapers across the United States. Newspapers in East Coast cities would publish the wire reports hours before newspapers in the middle of the country or on the West Coast. So a competing news service, International News Service, employed transcribers who would rewrite the Associated Press stories on the East Coast and send them to newspapers in the rest of the United States that were not members of the Associated Press collective. The Associated Press lost many members in the western United States because they saw that they could get almost the same information just a little later from the much cheaper International News Service. Lawyers for the Associated Press resurrected an old legal concept that would protect "hot news" from unfair competition. Ultimately, in 1918, the U.S. Supreme Court accepted this argument and established the concept of misappropriation. Misappropriation would occur if the plaintiff could demonstrate that it had spent money and effort creating the information, that the defendant took the information with very little original effort and to make money from the endeavor, and that the defendant harmed the plaintiff's ability to make money.

The concept of misappropriation has not been invoked successfully in recent years. In 1997 the National Basketball Association (NBA) tried to stop Motorola Corporation from transmitting game scores via a digital pager. The NBA argued that its games were copyrighted performances and the results of the games were creatively generated via the performance. The NBA also argued that Motorola misappropriated the score data in the same way that International News Service misappropriated the Associated Press stories. Federal courts, however, ruled that U.S. copyright law and its limits on the protection of facts preempted the common law misappropriation concept.

Europe has addressed the issue differently. Since 1996 the European Union has offered sui generis protection to databases to limit the potential misappropriation of all or part of a large collection of data. Database protection lasts for fifteen years after registration. But each time new data are added to the database the clock resets. So the protection is potentially unlimited in duration. There are many problems with this law. It is unclear how large a collection must be to qualify as a database. And it is unclear how much taking and at what frequency the taking must be to violate the law. Many bills have been drafted to add database protection to U.S. law since 1996 but none has passed. A rough consensus appears to exist that the American database industry needs no special protection.

Fashion

Few humans have more than two arms, two legs, and one head. So the creative template of clothing design is, quite simply, constricted by the standard form of the body. Yet within this template we have seen remarkable variation on themes like skirts, pants, shirts, blazers, hats, and underwear. All of this rampant creativity within the offices of designers in New York, Paris, Milan, and elsewhere has flourished with relatively weak or no intellectual property protection for fashion designs. As with so many forms of intellectual property, France and the United States have different values, different traditions, different political calculations, and different laws. France and the rest of Europe began expanding copyright protections to fashion design in the 1930s after designer Coco Chanel sued a clothing producer who had knocked off a number of her recent designs. The French court, ruling for Chanel and extending French copyright to fashion, declared her designs to be equivalent to a work of art. This matched the tradition of French and, by extension, European copyright law serving the interests of artists first and foremost, with much less concern for the utilitarian bargain between creators and the public interest that is reflected in American traditions.

The U.S. Congress has often considered implementing some sort of intellectual property protection for fashion design. But so far Congress has balked at the opportunity. American copyright law does not cover most aspects of fashion design because it does not protect items that have functional utility. Copyright could protect some design aspects such as logos or elaborate artwork printed or embroidered on a garment. But it would not protect the overall design of the garment. Trademarks, of course, play a key role in rewarding companies that clearly mark their products, such as Louis Vuitton or Nike. Specific technical advances such as advanced titanium alloys for eyeglasses would qualify for patent protection. But the shape and color of the glasses would not.

This lack of protection has allowed discount stores such as Zara, H&M, and Mango to copy fashion designs and sell garments similar to those available in upscale boutiques for much lower prices. This phenomenon has incensed many in the fashion world, but not all. Many fashion designers see copying as a key part of the overall culture of design and thus have argued that the fashion

10. The H&M fashion store on Knez Mihailova Street in Belgrade, Serbia. H&M is a Swedish company that has established a strong international following by copying the ideas of top-end designers, taking advantage of the lack of intellectual property protection for fashion designs.

industry in the United States actually benefits from the fact that designers must constantly generate bold, new designs as their previous designs meld into the cheaper markets. In addition, many designers like to revisit themes from past collections of their own houses and others. Copyright-like protection would limit the ability to revive designs and improvise upon a theme. Newness is what makes fashion exciting, and if designs enjoyed strong protection as they do in Europe, then there would be less incentive to create new designs. Successful designers could rest on their laurels and keep prices artificially high.

Traditional cultural expression versus the public domain

The opposite of intellectual property is the public domain. Expressions that are not protected by copyright law are free to be taken and to be used by anybody who wants to create a new expressive work. The material in the public domain is vast. It includes all facts, ancient myths, data, and books published before the twentieth century, works that were never protected by copyright at all, and expressions that have never been fixed in a medium. The public domain is a "commons." It is owned by no one. Therefore, it is owned by everyone. All substance within an intellectual or cultural commons is reused easily because it can never be exhausted. Rock 'n' roll artists used elements of Delta blues music from its public domain. And Walt Disney made his fortune and his company dominant by exploiting and revising public domain works such as *Cinderella* and *Snow White and the Seven Dwarfs*. Without a rich and plentiful public domain, new creators would have high transaction costs and other barriers to entry if they wish to converse by using the elements of a common culture. When the public domain fails to grow as copyrights fail to expire—as has been happening as legislators around the world have extended copyright terms—historians, poets, journalists, and songwriters find it harder to refer to stories and images that make up collective memory.

But there is a problem with the public domain. Those who create and wish to market goods and art that reflect traditions that are older than the twentieth century tend to find no help in the standard and established modes of intellectual property protection. Their work, no matter how creative or labor intensive or important to their cultural identity, is considered part of the grand global cultural commons. So multinational corporations can produce similar goods (pottery, cloth, garments, sculptures, jewelry, etc.) at lower prices. And these companies can leverage their marketing power better than small producers and merchants in poorer countries can.

Significantly for many of these cultural groups, replication of their traditional forms of cultural expression can be disrespectful of histories, identities, and religions as well. Intellectual property offers very little support for collective dignity. As several scholars of indigenous and traditional cultural production have argued in recent years, the cultural production of local communities is devalued not only because it is produced by marginal communities with no political power, but also because so much of that cultural production reflects traditions older than copyright. You cannot protect what has long been in the public domain without significantly revising the entire global intellectual property system.

Intellectual property does not treat all cultural expression equally. The weavers of Adinkra and Kente cloth in Ghana face competition from weavers working in Korea, China, India, and other parts of the world that host members of the Ghanaian diaspora. The patterns have a growing market. So many wish to mimic them. To accept that only the "new" shall be protected by intellectual property accepts the view that new is better than old. To mark Kente and Adinkra cloth as "traditional" is hegemonic. Traditions must reside permanently in the past, and they must be inferior to the "innovations" of the present and future. Importantly, the government of Ghana deftly markets the past. It distinguishes its traditional cloth as "authentic." It is hand-woven, not mass-produced. Global market logic demands that Ghana invest value in protecting its weavers' work as "traditional" because that is what differentiates it from the hundreds of other similar expressive goods flowing across trade channels. Efforts to create new forms of intellectual property law to protect "traditional knowledge" could merely reaffirm the permanent inferiority of creative works that have older origins and deeper modes of production. These works would be stuck just outside of modernity in an effort to fully exploit the modern market.

The very marginality of what has come to be known as the Traditional Cultural Expression movement—its reason for being—renders it peripheral to global discussions of cultural policy. Only when represented by a friendly and supportive nation state such as Canada or Australia do Traditional Cultural Expression movement members find their claims considered by policymaking officials. But this is state-driven action. The role of the state in the potential protection of traditional cultural expression presents many problems. How shall the state determine who is and who is not a member of a group trying to protect such expressions? What if the group is in opposition to the state? What if the group is split among factions? Who will determine the terms of licensing for songs, styles, and designs? The potential for censorship is daunting. So efforts toward a sui generis traditional cultural expression regime have been halting and have faced strong criticism. These efforts have generated some of the most heated and philosophically complicated debates within intellectual property.

More and miscellaneous

While the United States has as of 2016 resisted efforts to establish sui generis protection for fashion designs, it has not hesitated to protect other special interests when they have aligned with the legislative influence necessary for special treatment. The United States has special categories of law that protect the designs of boat hulls and semiconductors. Boat hull design is protected for a fixed term of ten years, and the law acts more like patent law than copyright law. It is a fairly broad and strong right that serves no general societal purpose. But it does reflect the power of a particular industry that garnered the ear of enough powerful legislators. The semiconductor protection right came from a moment of intense economic anxiety in the United States. In 1984 concern was acute that Japan and its state-supported technology sector would overtake the United States as the chief exporter of semiconductors. Semiconductors are engineered substances that can conduct electricity under some conditions but not others. This makes them governable and thus essential to the assembly of complex circuits of the sort used in computers and other advanced electronic machines. The advances in semiconductor technology since the 1980s have made much of the technological advances of recent decades possible. The United States sought any advantage it could generate to dominate the semiconductor trade. And research would demand significant resources. Because patent law demands novelty, the industry was concerned that small, incremental improvements in semiconductor technology would not qualify for patents. And because the design of the circuits drawn on the chip is utilitarian rather than creative, copyright would not work. With no faith that the semiconductor industry could do as well as the fashion industry has without intellectual property protection, the industry lobbied Congress for sui generis rights. The structure of the semiconductor protection right is a strange hybrid of elements of copyright and patent. It demands minimal novelty and allows for reverse engineering. But most of the exclusive rights available to a semiconductor developer resemble copyright.

The rise of these sui generis regimes and the proposals to create a new right for fashion in recent years reveal the extent to which intellectual property is a function more of politics than of carefully balanced policy decisions or high-minded theory. The older, more established, and classic areas of intellectual property—copyright, patent, and trademark—retain at least some measure of theoretical idealism in their rhetoric, if not their reality. But these other motley, sui generis intellectual property categories merely reflect the power of special interests.

Conclusion: The politics of resistance

Intellectual property exists as it does because powerful interests want it to exist. That is not the whole story. But it is the main story. Our global intellectual property systems reflect three centuries of changes in industries, politics, economics, and social values. In other words, intellectual property is fundamentally political. So what must we do as citizens of our various states to ensure that these systems work well for most people? How can we ensure that copyright fosters creativity at all levels without squelching it among some quarters? How can we ensure that new drug treatments come to market without the flexibility and dynamism that private enterprise can supply but still ensure that people who really need these treatments can afford them and that unprofitable treatments also emerge? How can we continue to reward companies that supply consistent, high-quality goods and services and ensure that consumers can find these goods with minimal effort and yet allow individuals and new businesses to use the symbols of the world around us to make meaning and communicate freely? These are difficult problems. Looking around the world, it is hard to conclude that we have established systems that satisfy these needs well. In the case of copyrights and patents, those who push for stronger protection are no happier with the status quo than those who push for weaker or more flexible protection.

Since about 2000 we have seen the rise of public awareness of intellectual property. As soon as millions of people around the world began connecting their computers and phones to global networks we all became deeply implicated in these systems. We all pay for them through the prices on goods and services. We all produce copyrighted material. We all copy copyrighted material without payment or permission. As goods, money, and people travel around the globe faster, farther, and more frequently than ever before, we have to confront not only challenges and opportunities that change culture. We also have to deal with communicable diseases never before seen and not fully understood. So we find a constant and growing need to develop new drugs to combat diseases like Ebola, malaria, influenza, and HIV/AIDS. But drug development is expensive. And so the treatments themselves are often prohibitively expensive to those in poorer parts of the world. Yet those poorer places often need the treatments more than the rest of us do. We have seen a "green revolution" in the biotechnology of agriculture—and the patents that support it—since the 1960s that has increased the production of food significantly. We are just now coming to terms with the social and cultural disruptions caused by lower commodity prices, global grain markets, and increased productivity that have driven people away from farms and to swelling urban slums everywhere from Brazil to Mexico City to Mumbai to Jakarta.

Understandably, we also have seen the rise of global activist movements devoted to fighting excessive intellectual property protection. These movements have been remarkably successful at rallying broad public concern to put pressure on legislators and companies. They have been disparate. But they have also coordinated some aspects of their approach. Hackers in Sweden and the Netherlands have launched political parties called Pirate Party to fight what they consider excessive copyright, surveillance systems, and intrusive technology policy. In the United States and Europe the "Free Culture" movement has rallied to oppose and strike down legislative proposals that would further empower

11. A woman protests the biotechnology and agriculture company Monsanto in New York City in May 2013. Her sign declares, "You Can't Patent Life."

copyright holders in their efforts to keep unauthorized copies of their works from circulating over digital networks. Law professor Lawrence Lessig inspired and led an effort to establish a new licensing system called "Creative Commons" that allows artists to signal to the world that people are free to make use of their material in creative ways without fear of legal retribution. Anti-biotechnology movements in India have invoked the spirit of Mohandas K. Gandhi to argue that genetically modified crops demand a high human cost to farmers in exchange for increased productivity and resistance to herbicides. And the global human rights movement has picked up the charge of pushing to reduce the price of essential pharmaceuticals in the developing world.

Many of these movements take inspiration from the Free and Open-Source Software movement that began in the 1980s among hackers and computer scientists who were frustrated at the rise of proprietary software. American computer scientist Richard Stallman proposed that hundreds of hackers contribute to a new free operating system that would do much the same work of the then-powerful, yet commercial, UNIX system. Once programmer Linus Torvalds from Finland began working on the core and key elements of such a system, he was able to guide a collaborative effort that eventually produced the LINUX operating system—still one of the most widely used computer systems in the world and the foundation of much of what works via Internet platforms. The key to having thousands of programmers contribute to such a project for no remuneration and have no company manage to take ownership of it was a brilliant copyright licensing scheme that Stallman devised: the General Public License. Through it, everyone who contributed source code to a free software project would agree to let anyone else copy or modify that code. The General Public License essentially locks the work open. No one who participates and contributes may shut anyone else out of the culture or the system. Trust grew among those who contributed to LINUX. A spirit of openness ruled. And the groups built impressive, complex software projects. Since the rise of LINUX and other free or open-source projects the General Public License model has worked for text-based projects like Wikipedia. And it serves as the inspiration for Creative Commons. Just as importantly, the ideology of openness and the strong resistance to intellectual property protection has spread to many other creative and political communities.

To varying degrees these movements have succeeded. In fact, the effort by human rights organizations, foundations, and the governments of India, Brazil, and Thailand have campaigned successfully to make available generic versions of drugs that fight the effects of HIV/AIDS. And the other elements of this effort that we can generally call the "Access to Knowledge" movement have succeeded at least in complicating the efforts of intellectual property holders to increase their protection. And they have all changed the conversation.

By the second decade of the twenty-first century we are just now achieving the level of awareness and concern necessary to forge the intellectual property systems that we deserve. The project that began in the eighteenth century with the Enlightenment is far from complete. It rests on faith that more knowledge shared by more people enables better decision making than corrupted or imperfect knowledge reserved to few. If we are to harness the best of the Enlightenment, its sense of the possibility of human beings lifting each other out of ignorance and pain through science and deliberation, we have to ensure that we all have access to the knowledge we need. But we also must have institutions that can afford to conduct the expensive research, production, and distribution that are necessary to produce blockbuster drugs and blockbuster films. Understanding intellectual property is a necessary, but it is far from a sufficient, step toward that goal.

Acknowledgments

I could not have started or completed this book without the guidance and patience of my editor at Oxford University Press, Nancy Toff. She approached me about the idea many years ago. And when I proceeded with fits and starts (mostly fits), she prodded me forward. Many others lent their research and insight and facilitated my acquiring the broad grasp of this subject that this book demanded. My agent, Sam Stoloff, once again cheered me on and prodded me when I needed it.

The community of intellectual property scholars is large and diverse. I could not list everyone who has proved influential in my studies. But I must give special thanks to a few. Ann Bartow has long been my close friend and advisor ever since I first stepped forward, a non-lawyer among law professors, and pretended to know something about copyright. Christopher Sprigman has had the greatest influence on me since I moved to the University of Virginia as one who has grown from a new colleague to a dear friend. The same can be said of Dotan Oliar and Zahr Said. Margo Bagley and Ruth Okediji taught me much about global patent law. Kembrew McLeod and Sonia Katyal clued me into the dynamics of pranks and culture jamming. Michael Brown's work made me think about the complexities of protecting "native culture." Michael Madison has opened my mind up to many new ways of thinking about copyrights and patents. And, as always, my role models and mentors in this field include James Boyle, Mark Lemley, Lawrence Lessig, Jessica Litman, Neil Netanel, and Pamela Samuelson. For the dozens of other great scholars who have been my friends, mentors, and inspirations, please see the list of important books at the end of this volume.

I am grateful to the students, alumni, faculty, and administration of the University of Virginia during the time it took to complete this book. Special thanks go to my colleagues in the Department of Media Studies. Judith McPeak, Krista Bajgier, and Barbara Gibbons helped me navigate the university and made my day job productive and fulfilling. Furious weeks of revision and editing of this book occurred during a wonderful visit to Microsoft Research in Cambridge, Massachusetts, where I benefited from feedback from Nancy Baym, Kevin Driscoll, Mary Gray, Jessa Lingel, Tressie McMillan Cottom, and Tarleton Gillespie. Most of all I have to thank two outstanding research assistants who helped me gather the raw materials for this project: Francesca Tripodi and Victoria Graham. And my students in my course "Copyright, Culture, and Commerce" all read the manuscript and gave me frank feedback.

My partner in life, Melissa Henriksen, has witnessed the composition of three of my four books. She still cannot understand why it takes so much more time to write a very short book than a significantly longer one. Fortunately, she has a sense of humor about it all. My daughter, Jaya, has had to endure yet another "grown-up book" in this one instead of the children's book I had promised her some years back. And our golden retriever, Butter, turned out to be no help at all.

I dedicate this book to my students at the University of Virginia. They have enhanced my curiosity for this subject by forcing me to confront their own inquisitive interests. Every semester they generate impressive insights and trenchant observations of how this tangle of laws, customs, and practices affect their lives and the creative worlds they seek to master. My brilliant students make my job beautiful and fun.

Further reading

Aoki, Keith. *Seed Wars: Controversies and Cases on Plant Genetic Resources and Intellectual Property*. Durham, NC: Carolina Academic Press, 2008.

Banner, Stuart. *Who Owns the Sky? The Struggle to Control Airspace from the Wright Brothers on*. Cambridge, MA: Harvard University Press, 2008.

Bartow, Ann. "Copyright Law and the Commoditization of Sex." In *Diversity in Intellectual Property*. Edited by Irene Calboli and Srividhya Ragavan, 339–65. Cambridge, UK: Cambridge University Press, 2015.

Behlendorf, Brian, Scott Bradner, Jim Hamerly, Kirk McKusick, Tim O'Reilly, Tom Paquin, Bruce Perens, et al. *Open Sources: Voices from the Open Source Revolution*. Edited by Chris DiBona, Sam Ockman, and Mark Stone. Sebastopol, CA: O'Reilly Media, 1999.

Bessen, James, and Michael James Meurer. *Patent Failure: How Judges, Bureaucrats, and Lawyers Put Innovators at Risk*. Princeton, NJ: Princeton University Press, 2009.

Boateng, Boatema. *The Copyright Thing Doesn't Work Here: Adinkra and Kente Cloth and Intellectual Property in Ghana*. Minneapolis: University of Minnesota Press, 2011. http://public.eblib.com/choice/publicfullrecord.aspx?p=718868.

Boldrin, Michele, and David K. Levine. *Against Intellectual Monopoly*. New York: Cambridge University Press, 2008.

Boldrin, Michele, and David K. Levine. "The Case against Intellectual Property." SSRN Scholarly Paper. Rochester, NY: Social Science Research Network, March 1, 2002. http://papers.ssrn.com/abstract=307859.

Boldrin, Michele, and David K. Levine. "The Case against Patents." *Journal of Economic Perspectives* 27, no. 1 (2013): 3–22. http://www.jstor.org/stable/41825459.

Boldrin, Michele, and David K. Levine. "The Economics of Ideas and Intellectual Property." *Proceedings of the National Academy of Sciences of the United States of America* 102, no. 4 (January 25, 2005): 1252–56. doi:10.1073/pnas.0407730102.

Boyle, James. *The Public Domain: Enclosing the Commons of the Mind.* New Haven, CT: Yale University Press, 2008.

Boyle, James. *Shamans, Software and Spleens: Law and the Construction of the Information Society.* Cambridge, MA: Harvard University Press, 1997.

Brown, Michael F. *Who Owns Native Culture?* Cambridge, MA: Harvard University Press, 2003.

Burk, Dan L., and Mark A. Lemley. "The Patent Crisis and How Courts Can Solve It." UC Irvine School of Law Review Working Paper No. 2009-8 (February 26, 2009). Available at SSRN eLibrary. http://papers.ssrn.com/sol3/papers.cfm?abstract_id=1349950.

Burk, Dan L., and Mark A. Lemley. *The Patent Crisis and How the Courts Can Solve It.* Chicago: University of Chicago Press, 2009.

Coombe, Rosemary J. *The Cultural Life of Intellectual Properties: Authorship, Appropriation, and the Law.* Durham, NC: Duke University Press Books, 1998.

Cowan, Jane K., Marie-Bénédicte Dembour, and Richard Wilson. *Culture and Rights: Anthropological Perspectives.* Cambridge, U.K.: Cambridge University Press, 2001.

David, Matthew. *Peer to Peer and the Music Industry: The Criminalization of Sharing.* London: SAGE, 2010.

Decherney, Peter. "Fair Use Goes Global." *Critical Studies in Media Communication* 31, no. 2 (2014): 146–52. doi:10.1080/15295036.2014.921321.

Decherney, Peter. *Hollywood's Copyright Wars from Edison to the Internet.* New York: Columbia University Press, 2012. http://public.eblib.com/choice/publicfullrecord.aspx?p=895258.

Dinwoodie, Graeme B., and Mark D. Janis. *Trademark Law and Theory: A Handbook of Contemporary Research.* Cheltenham, UK: Edward Elgar, 2008.

Doctorow, Cory. *Content: Selected Essays on Technology, Creativity, Copyright, and the Future of the Future.* New York: Tachyon, 2008.

Doern, G. Bruce, and Markus Sharaput. *Canadian Intellectual Property*. Toronto: University of Toronto Press, 2000.

Drahos, Peter, and John Braithwaite. *Information Feudalism: Who Owns the Knowledge Economy?* London: Earthscan, 2002.

Drahos, Peter, Ruth Mayne, and Oxfam GB. *Global Intellectual Property Rights: Knowledge, Access, and Development*. Basingstoke, UK: Palgrave Macmillan, 2002.

Ekstrand, Victoria Smith. *News Piracy and the Hot News Doctrine: Origins in Law and Implications for the Digital Age*. New York: LFB Scholarly, 2005.

"Fake Drugs: Poison Pills." *The Economist*, September 2, 2010. http://www.economist.com/node/16943895.

Fisher, William. "Two Thoughts about Traditional Knowledge." *Law and Contemporary Problems* 70, no. 2 (2007): 131–33. http://www.jstor.org/stable/27592183.

Gillespie, Tarleton. *Wired Shut Copyright and the Shape of Digital Culture*. Cambridge, MA: MIT Press, 2007. http://search.ebscohost.com/login.aspx?direct=true&scope=site&db=nlebk&db=nlabk&AN=190972.

Ginsburg, Jane C. "A Tale of Two Copyrights: Literary Property in Revolutionary France and America." *Tulane Law Review* 64, no. 5 (1990): 991–1032.

Ginsburg, Jane C., Jessica Litman, and Mary L. Kevlin. *Trademark and Unfair Competition Law: Cases and Materials*. New York: Foundation Press, 2001.

Goldstein, Paul. *International Copyright: Principles, Law, and Practice*. Oxford: Oxford University Press, 2001.

Hardin, Garrett. "The Tragedy of the Commons." *Science* 162, no. 3859 (December 13, 1968): 1243–48. doi:10.1126/science.162.3859.1243.

Heller, Michael A., and Rebecca S. Eisenberg. "Can Patents Deter Innovation? The Anticommons in Biomedical Research." *Science* 280, no. 5364 (May 1, 1998): 698–701. doi:10.1126/science.280.5364.698.

Heymann, Laura A. "Naming, Identity, and Trademark Law." *Indiana Law Journal* 86, no. 2 (2011): 382–445. Available at SSRN eLibrary. http://papers.ssrn.com/sol3/papers.cfm?abstract_id=1761614. Accessed February 15, 2011.

Hughes, Justin. "Champagne, Feta, and Bourbon - the Spirited Debate about Geographical Indications." *Hastings Law Journal* 58, no. 2

(2006): 299–. Available at SSRN eLibrary. http://papers.ssrn.com/sol3/papers.cfm?abstract_id=936362. Accessed September 20, 2011.

Hughes, Justin. "Notes on the Origin of Intellectual Property: Revised Conclusions and New Sources." *Cardozo Law Review* 33 (2011). Available at SSRN eLibrary. http://papers.ssrn.com/sol3/papers.cfm?abstract_id=1432860. Accessed September 20, 2011.

Hughes, Justin. "Political Economies of Harmonization: Database Protection and Information Patents." Cardozo Law School Public Law Research Paper No. 47 (July 8, 2002). Available at SSRN eLibrary. http://papers.ssrn.com/sol3/papers.cfm?abstract_id=318486.

Hunt, Geoffrey, and Michael D. Mehta. *Nanotechnology: Risk, Ethics and Law*. London: Earthscan, 2006.

Hyde, Lewis. *The Gift: Imagination and the Erotic Life of Property*. New York: Vintage Books, 1983.

Jaffe, Adam B., and Joshua Lerner. *Innovation and Its Discontents: How Our Broken Patent System Is Endangering Innovation and Progress, and What to Do about It*. Princeton, NJ: Princeton University Press, 2007. http://public.eblib.com/choice/publicfullrecord.aspx?p=713599.

Johns, Adrian. *Piracy: The Intellectual Property Wars from Gutenberg to Gates*. Chicago: University of Chicago Press, 2009.

Kapczynski, Amy. *Access to Knowledge in the Age of Intellectual Property*. New York: Zone Books, 2010.

Karaganis, Joe. *Media Piracy in Emerging Economies*. New York: Social Science Research Council, 2011. http://piracy.ssrc.org/the-report/.

Kernfeld, Barry. *Pop Song Piracy: Disobedient Music Distribution since 1929*. Chicago: University of Chicago Press, 2011.

Larkin, Brian. *Signal and Noise: Media, Infrastructure, and Urban Culture in Nigeria*. Durham, NC: Duke University Press, 2008.

Lemley, Mark A. "Property, Intellectual Property, and Free Riding." *Texas Law Review* 83 (2005): 1031. Available at SSRN eLibrary. http://papers.ssrn.com/sol3/papers.cfm?abstract_id=982977. Accessed September 20, 2011.

Lemley, Mark A. "The Surprising Virtues of Treating Trade Secrets as IP Rights." *Stanford Law Review* 61 (2008): 311–. Available at SSRN eLibrary. http://papers.ssrn.com/sol3/papers.cfm?abstract_id=1155167. Accessed September 20, 2011.

Lemley, Mark A., Michael Risch, Ted M. Sichelman, and R. Polk Wagner. "Life after *Bilski*." *Stanford Law Review* 63 (2011):

1315–47. Available at SSRN eLibrary. http://papers.ssrn.com/sol3/papers.cfm?abstract_id=1725009. Accessed September 20, 2011.

Lessig, Lawrence. *Code. Version 2.0.* New York: Basic Books, 2006.

Lessig, Lawrence. *Free Culture: The Nature and Future of Creativity.* New York: Penguin Press, 2004.

Lessig, Lawrence. *The Future of Ideas: The Fate of the Commons in a Connected World.* New York: Random House, 2001.

Loshin, Jacob. "Secrets Revealed: How Magicians Protect Intellectual Property without Law." Available at SSRN eLibrary. http://papers.ssrn.com/sol3/papers.cfm?abstract_id=1005564.

McKenna, Mark P. "A Consumer Decision-Making Theory of Trademark Law." SSRN Scholarly Paper. Rochester, NY: Social Science Research Network, January 19, 2012. http://papers.ssrn.com/abstract=1988521.

McKenna, Mark P. "The Normative Foundations of Trademark Law." SSRN Scholarly Paper. Rochester, NY: Social Science Research Network, December 30, 2010. http://papers.ssrn.com/abstract=889162.

McLeod, Kembrew. *Freedom of Expression: Resistance and Repression in the Age of Intellectual Property.* Minneapolis: University of Minnesota Press, 2007.

McLeod, Kembrew, and Rudolf E. Kuenzli. *Cutting across Media: Appropriation Art, Interventionist Collage, and Copyright Law.* Durham, NC: Duke University Press, 2011.

Miller, Toby, and George Yúdice. *Cultural Policy.* Thousand Oaks, CA: SAGE, 2002.

Mossoff, Adam. "A Stitch in Time: The Rise and Fall of the Sewing Machine Patent Thicket." SSRN eLibrary. http://papers.ssrn.com/sol3/papers.cfm?abstract_id=1354849.

Mossoff, Adam. "Who Cares What Thomas Jefferson Thought about Patents? Reevaluating the Patent 'Privilege' in Historical Context." *Cornell Law Review* 92, no. 5 (2007): 953–1012. Available at SSRN eLibrary. http://papers.ssrn.com/sol3/papers.cfm?abstract_id=892062. Accessed January 30, 2011.

Murray, Laura J., and Samuel E. Trosow. *Canadian Copyright: A Citizen's Guide.* Reprint. Toronto: Between the Lines, 2007.

Netanel, Neil. *Copyright's Paradox.* Oxford: Oxford University Press, 2008.

Okediji, Ruth L., and Margo A. Bagley. *Patent Law in Global Perspective.* Oxford: Oxford University Press, 2014.

Further reading

Patry, William F. *Moral Panics and the Copyright Wars.* New York: Oxford University Press, 2009.

Patry, William F. *How to Fix Copyright.* Oxford: Oxford University Press, 2011.

Patterson, Lyman Ray. *Copyright in Historical Perspective.* Nashville: Vanderbilt University Press, 1968.

Peñalver, Eduardo M., and Sonia K. Katyal. *Property Outlaws: How Squatters, Pirates, and Protesters Improve the Law of Ownership.* New Haven, CT: Yale University Press, 2010. http://search. ebscohost.com/login.aspx?direct=true&scope=site&db=nlebk&db= nlabk&AN=568251.

Raustiala, Kal, and Christopher Jon Sprigman. "The Piracy Paradox: Innovation and Intellectual Property in Fashion Design." *Virginia Law Review* 92 (2006): 1687–. Available at SSRN eLibrary. http:// papers.ssrn.com/sol3/papers.cfm?abstract_id=878401. Accessed September 20, 2011.

Raustiala, Kal, and Christopher Jon Sprigman. *The Knockoff Economy: How Imitation Spurs Innovation.* New York: Oxford University Press, 2012.

Rimmer, Matthew. *Intellectual Property and Biotechnology: Biological Inventions.* Cheltenham, UK: Edward Elgar, 2008.

Scafidi, Susan. *Who Owns Culture? Appropriation and Authenticity in American Law.* New Brunswick, NJ: Rutgers University Press, 2005. http://site.ebrary.com/id/10114304.

Schultz, Howard, and Joanne Gordon. *Onward: How Starbucks Fought for Its Life without Losing Its Soul.* New York: Rodale, 2011.

Sell, Susan. *Power and Ideas: North-South Politics of Intellectual Property and Antitrust.* Albany: State University of New York Press, 1998.

Sell, Susan. *Private Power, Public Law: The Globalization of Intellectual Property Rights.* Cambridge, UK: Cambridge University Press, 2003.

Shiva, Vandana. "Special Report: Golden Rice and Neem; Biopatents and the Appropriation of Women's Environmental Knowledge." *Women's Studies Quarterly* 29, nos. 1–2 (2001): 12–23. http:// www.jstor.org/stable/40004606.

Simon, Bryant. *Everything but the Coffee: Learning about America from Starbucks.* Berkeley: University of California Press, 2009.

Sinnreich, Aram. *Mashed Up: Music, Technology, and the Rise of Configurable Culture.* Amherst: University of Massachusetts Press, 2010.

Sinnreich, Aram. *The Piracy Crusade: How the Music Industry's War on Sharing Destroys Markets and Erodes Civil Liberties*. Amherst: University of Massachusetts Press, 2013.

Srinivas, Krishna Ravi. "Intellectual Property Rights and Traditional Knowledge: The Case of Yoga." *Economic and Political Weekly* 42, nos. 27–28 (2007): 2866–71. http://www.jstor.org/stable/4419783.

Sunder, Madhavi. *From Goods to a Good Life: Intellectual Property and Global Justice*. New Haven, CT: Yale University Press, 2012. http://site.ebrary.com/id/10568939.

Sunder, Madhavi. "The Invention of Traditional Knowledge." *Law and Contemporary Problems* 70, no. 2 (2007): 97–124. http://www.jstor.org/stable/27592181.

Trubek, Amy B. *The Taste of Place: A Cultural Journey into Terroir*. Berkeley: University of California Press, 2008.

Vaidhyanathan, Siva. *Copyrights and Copywrongs: The Rise of Intellectual Property and How It Threatens Creativity*. New York: New York University Press, 2003.

Vaidhyanathan, Siva. "Open Source as Culture—Culture as Open Source." *Open Source Annual*. Edited by Clemens Brandt. Berlin: Technische University, 2005. Available at SSRN eLibrary. http://papers.ssrn.com/sol3/papers.cfm?abstract_id=713044.

Vaidhyanathan, Siva. "The Anarchist in the Coffee House: A Brief Consideration of Local Culture, the Free Culture Movement, and Prospects for a Global Public Sphere." *Law and Contemporary Problems* 70, no. 2 (2007): 205–10. http://www.jstor.org/stable/27592187.

Vaidhyanathan, Siva. *The Anarchist in the Library: How the Clash between Freedom and Control Is Hacking the Real World and Crashing the System*. New York: Basic Books, 2004.

Vaidhyanathan, Siva. *The Googlization of Everything: (and Why We Should Worry)*. Berkeley: University of California Press, 2011.

van Overwalle, Geertrui, Esther van Zimmeren, Birgit Verbeure, and Gert Matthijs. "Dealing with Patent Fragmentation in ICT and Genetics: Patent Pools and Clearing Houses." *First Monday* 12, no. 6 (June 4, 2007). http://firstmonday.org/ojs/index.php/fm/article/view/1912.

Wayner, Peter. *Free for All: How LINUX and the Free Software Movement Undercut the High-Tech Titans*. New York: HarperBusiness, 2000.

Weber, Steven. *The Success of Open Source*. Cambridge, MA: Harvard University Press, 2005.

Willinsky, John. *The Access Principle: The Case for Open Access to Research and Scholarship.* Cambridge, MA: MIT Press, 2009.

Zimmerman, Diane Leenheer. "Fitting Publicity Rights into Intellectual Property and Free Speech Theory: Sam, You Made the Pants Too Long!" *DePaul Art & Entertainment Law Journal.* Available at SSRN eLibrary. http://papers.ssrn.com/sol3/papers.cfm?abstract_id=211789. Accessed September 20, 2011.

Zimmerman, Diane Leenheer. "Trade Secrets and the 'Philosophy' of Copyright: A Crash of Cultures." In *The Law and Theory of Trade Secrecy: A Handbook of Contemporary Research.* Edited by Rochelle L. Dreyfuss and Katherine J. Strandburg, 299–331. Cheltenham, UK: Edward Elgar, 2011. Available at SSRN eLibrary. http://papers.ssrn.com/sol3/papers.cfm?abstract_id=1438706. Accessed September 20, 2011.

Zittrain, Jonathan. *The Future of the Internet: And How to Stop It.* New Haven, CT: Yale University Press, 2009.

Zografos, Daphine. *Intellectual Property and Traditional Cultural Expressions.* Cheltenham, UK: Edward Elgar, 2012.

Websites

Canadian Intellectual Property Office
http://www.cipo.ic.gc.ca/eic/site/cipointernet-internetopic.nsf/eng/Home

Columbia University Copyright Advisory Office Guide to Copyright
http://copyright.columbia.edu/copyright/

Copyright Crash Course, from the University of Texas at Austin Libraries
http://copyright.lib.utexas.edu

Copyright for Librarians, from the Berkman Center for Internet and Society, Harvard University
http://cyber.law.harvard.edu/research/copyrightforlibrarians

Copyright Information and Resources from the University of Minnesota Libraries
https://www.lib.umn.edu/copyright

Copyright, Technology, and Access to the Law: An Opinionated Primer by James Grimmelmann
http://papers.ssrn.com/sol3/papers.cfm?abstract_id=1156829

Government of India Controller General of Patents Designs and Trademarks
http://www.ipindia.nic.in

Intellectual Property—An Overview, Government of the United Kingdom
https://www.gov.uk/intellectual-property-an-overview/overview

Intellectual Property—Wikipedia, the Free Encyclopedia
http://en.wikipedia.org/wiki/Intellectual_property

Intellectual Property, Stanford Encyclopedia of Philosophy
http://plato.stanford.edu/entries/intellectual-property/

Intellectual Property, from the Legal Information Institute, Cornell University Law School
http://www.law.cornell.edu/wex/intellectual_property

Intellectual Property Awareness Assessment, by the U.S. Patent and Trademark Office
https://ipassessment/uspto.gov/index.html

The Copyright Clearance Center
http://www.copyright.com

Understanding Intellectual Property, by IP Australia
http://www.ipaustralia.gov.au/understanding-intellectual-property/

What Is Intellectual Property? By the World Intellectual Property Organization
http://www.wipo.int/about-ip/en/

Index

Intellectual Property